MESSERSCHMITT BF110 AT WAR

Armand Van Ishoven

MESSERSCHMITT BF110 AT WAR

LONDON

IAN ALLAN LTD

2

Front cover, top:
Bf110C-2s of I/LG1 flying over Paris in 1940, after the French armistice.

Front cover, bottom:
Bf110C4, in early Battle of Britain unit altered camouflage. The basic scheme was RLM 70/71/65, but had RLM 65 extended up the fuselage sides and blended with a hand mottle of RLM 02. The machine belongs to I/ZG2 and carries non-standard unit markings (code letters).
Painting by Ian Huntley

1
Although the wartime censor did his best to 'remove' the unit emblem on the nearest aircraft, he forgot the unit code A2 on the aircraft in the background. This enables us to identify these Bf110D-0s as belonging to I/ZG52, shortly before the unit was redesignated II/ZG2.

2
A Kette of Bf110s of II/ZG2. Aircraft A2+BB is a Bf110C-4 and A2+BH a Bf110D-0. The Bf110D-0 in the background has the old camouflage pattern of black-green, dark green and a light blue, while the other aircraft are painted in the new scheme of dark green, RLM-grey and light blue. A2+BH was shot down on 7 September 1940 and crashed at Swan Lane, Downham Hall, Essex. Both crew members, Leutnant Abert and Unteroffizier Scharf, were killed.
Bundesarchiv

First published 1985

ISBN 0 7110 1504 X

Published by Ian Allan Ltd, Shepperton, Surrey; and printed by Ian Allan Printing Ltd at their works at Coombelands in Runnymede, England

Contents

Preface and Acknowledgements

What a joy it must have been to fly such a powerful twin-engined two-seater through the sky, at a time when the phrase 'fuel conservation' had not yet been invented and at a time when it was still possible to go to wherever you wanted without bothering with CTRs, TMAs, airways, FIRs and the like.

But at the same time, what a pity that such a sleek machine was designed and used for one purpose only: to wage war, to kill, maim and destroy.

War . . . man's destiny for centuries on end. And still some continue to try to impose upon others their religion, their economic or political system or simply their will. In the end the result is always the same: revolution, violence, war.

The day has yet to come when all this will fade into the past, and man at last will find a way to live in peace with his neighbour.

Acknowledgements

The author wishes to extend his grateful thanks for the help received while researching this book, especially to, the ladies Rosemarie Boos, Luise Leslie and Heidrun Steiner and to the following gentlemen: Bernd Barbas, Ewald Delbaere, Horst Diener, Gerhard Dubrow, J. Ellingworth, Wolfgang Falck, Adolf Galland, Walter Grabmann, Steven John Hall, Heinz Huhn, Hans-Joachim Jabs, Ab Janssen, Wilhelm Johnen, Arnold Klesse, Richard Lutz, Nicola Malizia, Huot Marchand, Victor Mölders, Hans Rasper, Oskar Rumler, Friedrich Runde, Alfons Schmitt, Kurt Schnittke, Werner Streib, John Stride, Hannes Trautloft, Ralph von Rettberg, Günther Wolf, Benno Wundshammer, Hermann Wurster, Willy Wüst, Paul Zorner.

I would also like to thank the following institutions for their assistance: Australian War Memorial, Canberra; Bundesarchiv, Koblenz and Freiburg; Deutsche Dienststelle WASt, Berlin; Fox Photos Ltd, London; Imperial War Museum, London; Messerschmitt-Bölkow-Blohm GmbH, Ottobrunn; Ministry of Defence, Air Historical Branch, London; Royal Air Force Museum, Hendon; Service Historique de l'Armée de l'Air, Vincennes; Volksbund Deutsche Kriegsgräberfürsorge e.V. Kassel.

One person who deserves a special mention is my friend George Van Acker. He spent much of his spare time in researching the photographs that appear in this book and in helping to write the captions. His devotion and help proved of great value and he deserves my deeply felt gratitude.

Armand van Ishoven

Glossary

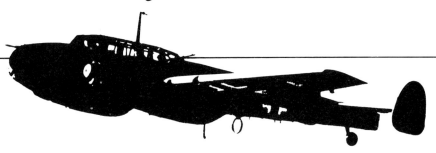

Der Adler	'The Eagle' — German magazine.
Alarmrotte	A *Rotte* on quick reaction alert.
Aufklärung	Reconnaissance.
Balkankreuz	(pl -e). The German cross; appeared on sides and wings of aircraft. See also *Hakenkreuz*.
Bereitschaft	Readiness.
Bf	Bayern Fabrik = built in Bavaria. Various Messerschmitt aircraft, for example the 108, 109, 110, are given the Bf designation. After 1938 the more usual Me was used.
Bodenstelle	Ground control.
Dackelbauch	Dackel = diminutive form of Dachshund. Bauch = belly. Name given to a non-jettisonable fuel tank hung from the belly of the Bf110.
Dunkelnachtjagd	German night fighting in searchlight zones was called *Hellenachtjagd* (illuminated night fighting) and when radar-directed became *Dunkelnachtjagd* (dark night fighting).
Erprobungsgruppe (ErpGr/ EGr)	Flight Testing *Gruppe*.
Fallschirmjäger	Paratroop.
Fernantrieb	Remote drive.
Fernaufklärungsgruppe	Long-distance reconnaissance *Gruppe*.
Gefechtstand	HQ.
Gefreiter	See 'Ranks'.
Geschwader	See 'Organisation'.
Gruppe	See 'Organisation'.
Haifisch	Shark.
Hakenkreuz	Swastika.
Hauptfeldwebel	See 'Ranks'.
Jagdbombergeschwader or *Jagdgeschwader* (JaboG/JG)	Fighter *Geschwader*.
Kampfgeschwader (KG)	Bomber *Geschwader*.
Kapitän	(pl -e). Captain.
Kette	See 'Organisation'.
Kommadore	Title given to *Geschwader* commander.
Kommandeur	Title given to the commander of a *Gruppe*.
Kommandant	Commandant.
Kompanie	Company.
Kriegsberichter	War reporter.

Lehrgeschwader (LG)	Training *Geschwader*.
Leutnant	See 'Ranks'.
Luftflotte	(pl -n). Air fleet. See 'Organisation'.
Luftwelt	'Air World' — a magazine.
LW-KBK	*Luftwaffe-Kriegsberichter-Kompanie*. A reporting unit.
Nachtjagdgeschwader (NJG)	Night-fighter *Geschwader*.
Nahaufklärungsgruppe	Close-range reconnaissance *Gruppe*.
Obergefreiter	See 'Ranks'.
Oberleutant (Oblt)	See 'Ranks'.
Oberwerkmeister	Chief Engineer.
Organisation	The Luftwaffe was directed from the Air Ministry and its flying units were divided into four *Luftflotten*, air fleets. The *Geschwader* was the largest tactical unit, it comprised three or four *Gruppen* with a *Stab* or HQ Flight. Its commander, usually a Major, Oberstleutant or Oberst, held the title of *Kommadore*. Each Gruppe had three or four *Staffeln* and a Stab. The Staffel was commanded by a Staffelkapitän who was usually an Oberleutant or Hauptmann. The Gruppe was commanded by a Hauptmann or Major who carried the title *Kommandeur*.
	The basic unit of the Staffel was the *Rotte*, a pair of aircraft — the leader *Rotteführer* and wing man. Two *Rotten* comprised a *Schwarm* — RAF equivalent, Flight — and there were three flights to a Staffel.
	The Geschwader were numbered, eg ZG52; the Gruppen had roman numerals and were represented thus, IV/KG52 or Stab/KG52; the Staffeln had arabic numbers.
Pioniere	Pioneers.
Ranks	

Luftwaffe	RAF Equivalent
Generaloberst	Air Chief Marshal
General der Flieger	Air Marshal
Generalleutnant	Air Vice Marshal
Generalmajor	Air Commodore
Oberst	Group Captain

3
The Bf110 had a very hard time during the Battle of Britain. This Bf110C-4 of an unknown unit returned from a flight over England with holes shot through its propeller blades, a damaged oil cooler intake and punctured tyres.

7

Oberstleutnant	Wing Commander
Major	Squadron Leader
Hauptmann	Flight Lieutenant
Oberleutnant	Flying Officer
Leutnant	Pilot Officer
Oberfeldwebel	Flight Sergeant
Feldwebel	Sergeant
Unteroffizier	Corporal
Gefreiter	Aircraftman 1st Class
Flieger	Aircraftman 2nd Class

Note: Kommandeur and Kommadore were titles and not ranks.

Reichsluftfahrtministerium (RLM)	Air Ministry.
Reihenbildner (Rb)	Camera.
Ritterkreuz	Knight's Cross.
Rotte	See 'Organisation'.
Rüstzsatz	Jettisonable fuel tank.
Schwarm	See 'Organisation'.
Schnellkampfgeschwader (SKG)	Fast bomber *Geschwader*.
Sitzbereitschaft	'Seated readiness' — waiting in the aircraft for an alarm take-off.
Stab	Staff/headquarters.
Staffel	(pl -n). See 'Organisation'.
Stammkennzeichen	Identification symbol.
Sturzkampfgeschwader (STG)	Dive bomber *Geschwader*.
Unteroffizier (Uffz)	(pl -e). See 'Ranks'.
Werksnummer (WNr)	Works serial number.
ZbV	*Zur besonderen Verwendung* 'for special purpose'.
Zerstörer	Nickname of the Bf110, literally 'Destroyer'. Also used to denote twin-engined fighters.
Zerstörergeschwader (ZG)	Twin-engined fighter *Geschwader*.
Zwilling	The double machine gun at the rear of the Bf110 cockpit.

4
Well-known view of Bf110E-1/U2, 2J+AP, of the 6th Staffel of II/ZG1. This type of aircraft carried a crew of three: pilot, control-officer and gunner. A *Spanner-Anlage* (infra-red sensor) was installed in the cockpit, being operated by the *Leitoffizier* (control-officer). The fairing beneath the white dot on the fuselage, behind the rear of the cockpit, is an opening used for cockpit ventilation. II/ZG1 saw extensive action in Russia and was later transferred to the Italian front and the French Atlantic coast at Brest.

First Flight

The first Bf109 prototype made its first flight on 28 May 1935 at the hands of BFW Chiefpilot Hans-Dietrich Knoetzsch. After the much publicised landing accident of Bf109-V1 at the RLM's testing centre at Rechlin, Knoetzsch left the Messerschmitt firm. So when the Bf110 prototype was ready for its first flight the honour of making it fell to Dr Ing Hermann Wurster who had been Chief Test Pilot of BFW since 1 January 1936. This first flight of Bf110 V1 (WNr 868, civil registration D-AHOA) took place on 12 May 1936 at Augsburg airfield almost a year after that of Bf109 V1. It lasted 10 minutes and more than 40 years later, Dr Ing Wurster told the author about that first flight:

'Prof Messerschmitt, Director Hentzen and many other members of the firm were present on the airfield. First of all I did some taxi-trials in order to test manoeuvrability on the ground. Take-off was uneventful. This first flight was no simple circuit. For safety's sake I climbed to 2,000m to do some stall tests. First of all I tested the efficiency of the ailerons, the rudder and the elevator. Then I tested the stability about the vertical, the horizontal and the transverse axis. Lastly I tested the stall characteristics while the engines were idling.

'I did this mostly to find out what was the safe speed on finals. In those days, the approach speed had to be found out by the test-pilot, today it is given by the aerodynamics bureau!

'The aircraft showed good control efficiency which emboldened me, even at this very early stage, to do some rather

5
Dr Ing Herman Wurster first took Bf110 V3 to the air on 24 December 1936, taking off at 11.05hrs and landing at 11.18hrs. The aircraft bore WNr 870. The photo shows Wurster at the controls of the aircraft as yet without any markings. Its registration D-ATII was applied at a later stage.

steep turns. Stability around the three axes was perfect. When stalling the aircraft did not fall off one wing but pitched down straight forward. The landing too was uneventful, although after touching down I found that the undercarriage brakes were too weak and that idling was too high. I had to switch off the ignition so that I didn't run into a hangar.

'Once I had stopped, Prof Messerschmitt and Director Hentzen congratulated me for the good landing. My first verbal report to Prof Messerschmitt after landing was thus: "Controls of the 110 are very good in both horizontal flight and while turning. When stalling the aircraft shows no tendency dangerously to fall off a wing or to spin. The flaps are adequate for landing. I believe that we will not have any difficulties with the 110 as concerns handling characteristics."

'Then I turned towards Chief Engineer Asam and said: "The brakes do not work too well; the air must be taken out and they have to be adjusted. Idling speed of the engines is too high and must be regulated to a lower level."

'I did not retract the undercarriage during this first flight. This only took place during

6
Bf110 V5 D-AAHI, WNr 911, made its first flight on 15 March 1938, taking off at 17.07hrs and landing again at 17.15hrs. Bf110 V7, WNr 917, painted in Luftwaffe markings, flew for the first time on 19 April 1938 from 14.07hrs until 14.21hrs. Both aircraft were flown by Hermann Wurster and were the prototypes for the B-0 series of which only 10 aircraft were actually built. Two Junkers Jumo 210G engines were installed and the redesigned nose section was aerodynamically refined. Two 20mm MG FF cannon were mounted on the floor in the rear part of the cockpit, firing through two openings in the lower part of the nose section. The Bf110B-0 depicted has had its cannon openings 'removed' by the wartime censor.

the second flight on 25 May 1936. We did not have any trouble with it or, indeed, with the DB600 engines, although early on there were some minor problems with engine cooling.

'In my flying logs the abbreviation "Bf" was replaced by "Me" from 23 May 1936. The official change from Bf to Me followed after the change of name from Bayerische Flugzeugwerke AG to Messerschmitt AG in July 1938.

'On 27 August 1936, the Chief of the Technical Department, Ernst Udet, visited us in order to have a look at the 110. I demonstrated aerobatics with the 110 V1 and he was visibly impressed and wanted to see a dog-fight demonstration between the 109 and the 110. Udet took the 109 and I the 110. We agreed that we would meet over the airfield at 1,000m and start a dogfight.

'During the ensuing fight it became clear that the Me110 could fly as tight a turn as the Me109. Indeed, Udet did not succeed in getting me into his sights. The Me109 could not shoot down the Me110 in an aerial fight. Due to the good stalling characteristics of the Me110 it did not fall off the outer wing even during the steepest of turns while this was possible with the Me109. Udet was enthusiastic about the 110.'

According to Herr Wurster's flight logs he made the first flight with the second prototype, Bf110 V2 (WNr 869, D-AQYE) on 24 October 1936. Then the aircraft was made ready for the acceptance tests at the *Erprobungsstelle* Rechlin. On 14 January 1937 he flew the aircraft to Rechlin and on the 22 January he demonstrated aerobatics during a first flight and a full-power 20deg dive during a second flight that day. The next day he demonstrated stalls and one-turn spins followed by measured take-offs and landings with maximum flying weight.

Herr Wurster made the first flight with Bf110 V3 (WNr 870, D-ATII) on 24 December 1936. Bf110 V4 (WNr 910 D-AISY) followed on 21 January 1938 and Bf110 V5 (WNr 911 D-AAHI) on 15 March of that year.

After WNr 917 the Bf110s no longer carried civil registrations but Luftwaffe markings.

7
Several Bf110B-1s were used as trainers. The armament was reduced to four MG17 nose-mounted machine guns but in some instances the armament was removed altogether (Bf110B-3) and improved radio and blind-flying equipment installed. This Bf110B-3, WNr 1736, is seen in company of an Italian Regia Aeronautica Cant Z-1007bis 'Alcione'. In the background a Heinkel He51A-1 is landing. *Nicola Malizia*

Stealing a Bf110

Secrecy surrounded the Luftwaffe's new aircraft for a long time. Despite the fact that the first prototype first flew on 12 May 1936, little or nothing was known about it outside of Germany when Général Vuillemin, Commander-in-Chief of the French Armée de l'Air visited Germany during the second half of August 1938. During his visit he was shown one of the earliest Bf110s and he was very much intrigued by it.

Even its first public appearance a few weeks later during the 'Army Day' of the 'Reich's Party Day' in early September 1938 at Nuremberg did not reveal any significant details. It was only after the Bf110 had been mentioned in *The Aeroplane* of 28 September that the German aviation press gave some details about it. . . taken from *The Aeroplane!*

Early in 1938 French specialists had had the opportunity to examine and fly a Condor Legion Bf109B which had fallen into the hands of the Republicans and so the Bf109 held few secrets for the French. Not so with the Bf110 which was not used during the Spanish Civil War, and kept its secrets. Even the authoritative Jane's *All the World's Aircraft* in its December 1939 issue — after World War 2 had started — was obliged to print that the Me110 was a twin-engined monoplane 'of which very little information is available for publication'.

After Vuillemin's visit the French desperately wanted to know more about the Bf110; so they made a plan. The plan was simply to steal a Bf110 and have it flown to a secret French airfield. The man who was to work out the plan was Colonel André Sérot, *Chef des Services de Renseignement Air* based at Belfort, a French town near the German and Swiss border. The man who was actually to steal the Bf110 was Franz Xaver Öttil, a pilot recently fired from the Luftwaffe for disobedience. (Flying a Luftwaffe biplane he had hit the roof of his family's farm!) Unfortunately both actors of the drama are no longer with us to tell the story. Franz Öttil died in the attempt to fly the Bf110 to France, and André Sérot was murdered in Jerusalem in September 1946 at the side of Count Folke Bernadotte, mediator of the United Nations.

So, who was Franz Öttil?

Franz was born in Türckheim, in Bavaria, some 60km west of Munich, on 2 January 1914. Early in 1935 Franz joined the Luftwaffe and on 3 June of that year obtained his military pilot's licence (*Militärischer Flugzeugführerschein*). On 1 October 1937 he obtained his *Blindflugschein* (IFR rating) at the Perleberg Flying School. Autumn 1937 saw him at the *Kampffliegerschule* Tutow (bombing school) and in early 1938 he joined StG 2 'Immelmann' at Schwerin. By then he was a Luftwaffe-Unteroffizier, but in the course of 1938 he was fired from the Luftwaffe for disobedience.

On 10 December 1938 he obtained a German passport valid not only for Germany but for Italy, Rumania, Czechoslovakia, Bulgaria and Hungary as well. Two days later, on 15 December, he joined the NSFK, the state organisation patronising all aerial sports. Less than a month later from 7 to 15 January 1939 he made a journey to Yugoslavia, rather surprising for a young German at that time. Five months later he succeeded in getting a job with the Messerschmitt firm at Augsburg, in doing so keeping secret that he had been a pilot. On 24 April 1939 he was taken in to service by Messerschmitt as a *Start Monteur* (starting mechanic) in the *Serieneinfliegerei* (series test flying). Three weeks later, on 10 May 1939, he took off from Augsburg airfield in the stolen Bf110C-1, WNr 979.

Kurt Schnittke was at that time also working in the *Einfliegerabteilung* (testing department) at Augsburg. (He was later to become flying mechanic to the legendary Ernst Udet.) Nearly 40 years later he recalled:

'Augsburg, Serieneinfliegerei, Werk III (Plant 3) at around 12.30hrs. The first workers' shift was just returning from lunch as the second shift left for its meal. A Bf110 was taxying towards the Kompensierschiebe, on which the whole compass installation and radio-direction finding equipment was tested. But suddenly the pilot applied full power and the Bf110 took off. Everybody looked at each other. Who was in the aircraft? All mechanics were quickly summoned together and it was discovered that Franz Öttil, the mechanic of the aircraft which had just taken off, was missing.

'Flugkapitän Willi Stör, in charge of the Serieneinfliegerei, Ingenieur Piel and Meister Gerstenacker hurriedly drove to air traffic control but when they reported that a Bf110 had been stolen their report was taken as a joke. Stör wanted to take-off in a Bf109 to pursue Öttil but there was no aircraft available. More than half an hour had elapsed before the air traffic controller was willing to report the theft of a Bf110 and he only did it then on condition that Willi Stör took responsibility for the report.

'After the abduction all Messerschmitt aircraft to be tested were equipped with a large steel clamp that fitted over the tailplane and which was closed by a security lock. In that way the aircraft could be taxied and even if full power was applied, the aircraft could not take-off. Only the pilots had a key.'

In the meantime Franz Öttil had taken off in the Bf110 without a parachute, sitting on a cushion. After having flown 40km to the southwest, towards Bad Wörishofen, not far from his parental farm, he landed on a sports field. . . where his older brother Johann stood waiting with a number of petrol cans. The two brothers poured the fuel into the Bf110, and then both climbed into the aircraft and took-off.

What happened next nobody will know for sure.

The next witness of the drama was Raymond Guinchard, a teacher at the small French village of Villers-sous-Chalamont, north of Lausanne and hardly 100km from Belfort, where Colonel Sérot was based. Guinchard recalled:

'I was taking a walk at about 6 o'clock in the evening when suddenly I heard the noise of an aircraft coming from the east. For a few minutes it circled above me and then suddenly I heard it dive, its engine now and then faltering. I couldn't see a thing as the fog was so dense and I threw myself flat on the ground. I have no idea how high the aircraft was when it passed above me but a few seconds later I heard an explosion and then, wafted by the wind, the smell of burning.

'I ran in the direction the explosion had come from and suddenly saw the tail of an aircraft, with a swastika on it. Later on I realised that I had been only 250m from the point of impact.'

Even closer than Guinchard was Edouard Courtet and his sister, who were taking cattle towards a meadow only 100m away.

8
The eventful flight of the Ottil brothers on 10 May 1939 ended in tragedy. Due to the heavy fog the pilot, Xaver Ottil, lost his bearings and was forced to fly lower and lower to find a suitable place for an emergency landing. At around 18.00hrs their Bf110C-1, WNr 979, hit the ground and exploded on impact; both Xaver and his brother Johann were killed instantly. The aircraft came down near Villers-sous-Chalamont, Doubs, parts of it being strewn all over the field, as is evident from the photographs taken after the crash. Although this crash meant the end of WNr 979, the aircraft would be mentioned one more time. The Messerschmitt, Augsburg, record, dated 3/7/40, has the following sentence: 'Bf110C-1, 102-102, DB601A (including WNr 979, aircraft destroyed)'.

They found two horribly mutilated corpses. . . the brothers Öttil.

Then came the crowds, the souvenir hunters and, finally, the Gendarmes. Later the mortal remains of Franz and Johann were transported to Villers-sous-Chalamont where a 'Chapelle Ardente' at the local fire station was set up. On 19 May, representatives of the German Embassy came to take the bodies back to Augsburg. Kurt Schnittke takes up the story:

'As soon as the report of the theft was sent out there were questionings by the Gestapo. The next day we heard a message over the radio that an aircraft of unknown nationality had crashed in the Vosges in France and we realised that it must be our Bf110. A few days later two coffins arrived bedecked with flowers and a French tricolour. We were astonished that there was a second body!'

In France the scattered remains of the Bf110 were carefully examined by members of the Inspection Générale Technique de l'Air and some parts, amongst them one of the engines, were sent to the Service de l'Armement for laboratory tests. The minute examination resulted in a report on the *'enseignements d'ordre technique et tactique tirés de l'examen de l'appareil'*, the technical and tactical lessons taken from the examination.

9
The mortal remains of Xaver and Johann were removed from the site of the crash and transported to Villers-sous-Chalamont. There, at the local fire station, a 'Chapelle Ardente' has been furnished; between the two coffins is a wreath from the German Embassy in Paris.
Photographs in this chapter via Huot Marchand

Some of the Bf110's secrets had been discovered!

Needless to say, the local French newspapers commented extensively upon the mysterious accident, even if officially the Press was asked to play the affair down and not to mention that a military aircraft was involved. It was a considerable source of embarrassment to both countries. The French had planned a secret mission that would have left the Germans completely in the dark — after all there could have been no proof that the aircraft had come down in France. However, the fact that the aircraft crashed in a populated area prevented the secrecy being maintained.

The official German explanation of the crash was that a training aircraft had got lost in the dense fog. Two months later, on 28 June 1939, Major von Cramon, Chief of the German Air Ministry department in charge of foreign Air Attache relations, summoned the young Captain Stehlin, attached to the French Air Attache:

'It is more than two months since the accident and yet we have still not been able to recover our aircraft. We understand perfectly that your technical department has an interest in it and wants to learn about the novelties it may present but it could have acted with more tact. . . .

'Everything that has happened is deeply regrettable. We have the impression that your official services do everything which lies in their power to poison the relations between our two countries. One of these days that will end in catastrophe . . . '.

Many mysteries surround the theft of the Bf110 even to this day, even after extensive historical research. How did the French induce the two young Germans to steal an aircraft and try to deliver it to France? Why did Franz Öttil travel to Yugoslavia four months before the abduction?

One intriguing fact that emerged when researching this story involved Franz Öttil's sister who is still alive and living in Bavaria. One of the many letters the author wrote to various sources was the first sign of her brothers that she received since they disappeared in May 1940. After the abduction she was interrogated by the Gestapo but apparently nobody ever told her that the mortal remains of her brothers had been returned to Augsburg. For all those years she had been ignorant of where they had been buried.

10

On 3 July 1939 an exhibition was held at the Rechlin Test Centre. Shown were various new aircraft types, aero-engines, aircraft armament and equipment, etc. Bf110B-0 D-AAPY which belonged to the Rheinmetall firm and was equipped with a 30mm Rheinmetall MK 101 cannon beneath the fuselage, was shown to the distinguished visitors. This armament was to be used against tanks and surfaced submarines. The observer-gunner could reload the cannon from inside the cockpit. The trials were very satisfactory and effective and in the end this form of armament was installed on Bf110C-6 and Henschel Hs129B-1/R2 aircraft. The Bf110C-6s were used in the bomber interceptor rôle but not much is known about their

effectiveness under combat conditions. This kind of armament would, however, reappear on Bf110s in late 1942, albeit in a different form. Some Bf110G-2/R1s, equipped with a fuselage-mounted 37mm BK3.7 (Flak 18) cannon, were used as daytime bomber interceptors but, as the Luftwaffe soon found out, with disastrous results. Here D-AAPY is seen along with high-ranking visitors attending the exhibition. From left to right: Generalluftzeugmeister Ernst Udet, unknown, the Führer Adolf Hitler, Reichsmarschall Hermann Göring, Generaloberst Erhard Milch, unknown, Generaloberst Wilhelm Keitel, unknown, Generalingenieur Roluf Lucht, Reichsleiter Martin Bormann, unknown and SS-Gruppenführer Theodor Eicke. *Bernd Barbas*

11

12

On 16 July 1940 Generalluftzeugmeister Ernst Udet became the user of Bf110D-0 VF+HP, WNr 3354; this aircraft replaced his ageing Bf110C-1, GK+AY WNr 945 and was stationed at Tempelhof airfield. The aircraft had been used at Tarnewitz for armament

trials. Udet's faithful companion on all of his flights was his mechanic, Gefreiter Kurt Schnittke. Udet saw to it that a rear-view mirror was installed INSIDE the cockpit. Very few people knew its function. During a flight Udet now and then liked to take a sip of Cognac from the small flask he carried and he

thought it only right that his flying mechanic did the same. However, when the mechanic took a sip it made a noise in the microphone which could be worrying — but when he saw Schnittke in the mirror taking a sip, Udet could be happy that nothing was amiss.

11

In 1937, the Germans envisaged a further development of the Bf110. It was already clear to them that the short-range Zerstörer, which performed the role of dive-bomber, was in need of a more powerful rearward-firing armament. The single rearward-firing MG15 was inadequate — the Battle of Britain would make this very clear to the Germans — and something had to be done to rectify this. In late 1939 Bf110C-1 BA+CP was used as a test-bed for the FA12 (*Fernantrieb Typ 12*). One *Ferngerichtete Drehringlafette* FDL 81Z gun-barbette was mounted on top and another beneath the fuselage, each of them containing a 7.92mm MG81Z *Zwilling* machine gun. Trials soon revealed that it was utterly impossible for a crew member, performing the tasks of wireless-operator, navigator and gunner, to scan the sky for enemy aircraft creeping up from behind, by looking through a periscope. It was evident that the only way to look for enemy aircraft was by means of the naked eye and that the sole purpose of the periscope was that of an aiming device. Since no room was left for a third crew member, production of the Bf110 outfitted with this type of armament was not taken up. *J. Ellingworth*

Zerstörer over Poland

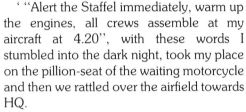

13
The German attack on Poland is imminent. One of the Bf110Cs of I/ZG1 is being readied for its flight against the enemy. One of the barrels of the nose-mounted 7.92mm MG17 machine guns is being replaced.

' "Herr Oberleutnant, time to get up. Briefing at 04.00hrs for the Staffel leaders at HQ. Mission starts at 04.45hrs." A torch shone at me and called me back to grim reality after a short stretch of sleep. In the pale light I recognised the face of the Hauptfeldwebel, who thoughtful as ever, hadn't woken me up one moment earlier than necessary. A quick glance at my watch: 03.40hrs.

' "Alert the Staffel immediately, warm up the engines, all crews assemble at my aircraft at 4.20", with these words I stumbled into the dark night, took my place on the pillion-seat of the waiting motorcycle and then we rattled over the airfield towards HQ.

'The greetings of the Staffel leaders were answered by a curt "Good morning" from the commander who was studying a map of Poland by the light of a candle. The pale light of dawn in the east announced a new day. Everybody waited tensely for the new orders.

' "Our mission — the Gruppe will start free hunting in the Lodz area. The centre of the activity will be at the airfield of Dalikow, some 28km NW of Lodz at 04.45hrs. The second Staffel will lead, the first and third will fly on either side, higher and to the rear. Any questions? Thank you and *Weidmannsheil* (good hunting)."

'We left feeling happy — at least our sincerest wish had been fulfilled: free hunting. Day after day the Staffel had been ordered into the air time after time to fly cover for the bomber formations. It is certainly a worthy mission to protect our comrades against enemy fighters, but our passionate wish was to be able to find the enemy ourselves, to attack and to destroy him. Today we could do just that — near Lodz of all places.

'To us Lodz had become synonymous with heavy anti-aircraft fire and enemy fighters. It was at Lodz that the Polish fighters had taken us for bombers and had attacked us from the front, only to be taken by surprise when we greeted them with our machine guns and cannon, and shot them down.

'It was at Lodz that we lost two of ours during a heated combat with six Polish fighters of which two also were shot down. One of our own had to land near the city because its engines had been shot up. For three weeks we didn't hear anything from its crew and we feared for the worst until at last the wounded pilot was freed from Polish captivity and returned home; his wireless operator had been killed. All these facts and much more had made Lodz a very special place for us and now it was our target.

'In the meantime it was getting lighter in the east. Morning mist floated over the airfield. The senior officer called the roll of the assembled crews. I gave the necessary orders curtly and everyone sprinted towards their aircraft, shouting a last joke at each other or wishing well to a comrade. Everyone knew that today was the day that we had to prove our capability, the strength of our belief in our weapons, the high degree of our training and the right spirit of the fighter pilot.

'Soon my aircraft rolled over the airfield and took off. It was still dark enough to necessitate use of navigation-lights so that the Staffel could formate more quickly. "All stations taken up", I heard through the WT from my wireless operator, reporting that all aircraft of the Staffel had closed in and were flying the correct formation. To our rear and higher than ourselves I could see the two other Staffeln. I armed my cannon and machine guns and turned on the gunsight; all was now ready.

'Our first target was the airfield at Dalikow. The attacks during the first days had been so devastating that we had gained aerial supremacy and now we had to attack ground positions. Slowly the land below us glided past. Mistbanks covered the lower lying parts of the country and made navigation difficult as did the first rays of the morning sun. We should by now be almost above our target so I put away the maps and kept my eyes peeled.

'We were flying at only 1,800m and suddenly the leader of my second Rotte opened his throttles, accelerated, closed on my aircraft, waved towards the right and then swung down at once, followed by his Rotte. I followed him and saw below a three-engined Fokker, a fat morsel. The second Rotte was already on him and I watched the tracers punching into the aircraft's fuselage. The Fokker slowly started to dive . . . the leading Bf110

overshot the enemy aircraft and his wingman had a go. I too dived towards it — and saw it crash into the ground and burst into flames. The Rottenführer had got his first victory! But what a very large field the wreck was lying in . . . and there were two more Fokkers, well camouflaged, standing on it . . .

'We'd found the airfield and the rest of the Staffel attacked — the next aircraft, two, three, four, immediately dived down. The first volleys hit the parked aircraft and flames several metres high shot upwards from their fuselages.

'Our first target had been destroyed but we had to keep on going; the Poles mustn't be given any rest. There must be other targets. But where? We didn't bother with the Polish machine guns which fired from their camouflaged positions around the airfield — the morning hunt wasn't over and we were still looking for more big game. I climbed to 1,500m, signalled to the Staffel to formate, to look for further action.

'There! What was that flickering in front of us? It looked suspicious to me and I dived towards it. It was a PZL P23 bomber flying towards me at a lower altitude. I

14
A member of the ground crew, heavily loaded with a cartridge belt, hopes to get relieved of his burden as soon as possible. The belt contains 1,000 rounds of 7.92mm ammunition and one was needed for each of the Bf110's four nose-mounted MG17 machine guns.

slammed the throttles shut, pulled the aircraft round and dived. I could clearly make out the red-and-white checkerboard, the Polish cockades, on its wings and fin. The Polish observer was already firing at me, but he aimed poorly. His tracers flashed past me. At that same moment I got him in my sights. A small correction — now — I pushed the button, my machine guns hammered away — a flame stabbed out — he exploded and as I roared away above him he disappeared below as a sinking ball of fire, before crashing in a freshly sowed field.

'My radio operator congratulated me and then pointed to the right. A second aircraft of the same type passed below us, with one of ours — piloted by Leutnant F — sitting on its tail. He shot, the Pole started burning and then fell and crashed . . .

'I wheeled about and saw another PZL behind me. Then he disappeared in spouting flame, a smoke trail, a crash. His victor, Leutnant U, recognised my aircraft and came towards me and the Staffel formated again. It was 05.42hrs. Six pillars of smoke marked our path. We scanned the earth and the sky; empty . . .

'A glance at the fuel gauge told me that we had to start thinking about flying home, but not before carrying out some "minor jobs". We didn't have to look long to find them. The station of Idunkla-Wola seemed to be extremely busy. Locomotives were being shunted about, freight and military transport trains were rolling along and an armoured train gave us the challenge of more action. It only took a moment to see the target, and then the whole Staffel attacked it. Fire from machine guns and from light AA guns met us, but we had already had enough practice "picking" locomotives in the last few days. Smoke and steam shot out from the trains as if their souls were escaping towards the heavens. Here a locomotive exploded; there a goods train was burning. We climbed upward to dive again, this time at a railway yard — apparently a carriage works. The volleys smashed into the roof, dirt flew about,

15
Shortly after 04.00hrs on the morning of 1 September 1939, Luftwaffe units started their air attack on Poland. Among the units involved was 2/ZG76. Headed by the Bf110C-1 flown by the Staffelkapitän, Oberleutnant Wolfgang Falck, they begin to move in.

16
Polish pilots of 113 ('Owls') Squadron of the 1st Regiment salute their squadron leader after receiving their instructions. Along with four other squadrons the unit belonged to the Pursuit Brigade and was stationed near Warsaw. The aircraft are PZL P-11a fighters, popularly known as the *Jedenastka* (the Eleventh). The excellent manoeuvrability and sturdy structure made it a dreaded opponent, especially when flown by skilled pilots. These pilots put up a valiant battle against the invaders but in the end could not resist the overwhelming power of the German Luftwaffe.

smoke here, a flame there. The ground below us offered a spectacle of chaos and destruction.

'Finally the attack was over and I got the Staffel together for the flight home. After a flight of 2½ hours, which had taken us far into enemy country, the Staffel landed at its advanced airstrip. The aircraft rolled to their dispersals, the ground personnel surrounded the crews eager to hear the stories of success and adventure. Those who looked after our aircraft, weapons, engines and wireless sets, also played their part in our victory.

'The red ladybird with the seven black dots, the Staffel insignia which was carried on the left side of each of our aircraft, had proven itself once more.'

This report was written in 1939 by Oberleutnant Falck, Staffelkapitän of 2/ZG76 and printed in the booklet *Schlag auf Schlag*, a 'report in words and pictures' about the German Luftwaffe in Poland. It was published by Dr H. Eichelbaum, a Major in the RLM (Reichsluftfahrtministerium), in 1939.

Forty years later, Herr Wolfgang Falck, now working for a large US aerospace company, gave the author permission to use this text again. From the beginning of the war until June 1943 he flew some 90 missions with the Bf110, obtaining seven victories. He then served in staff positions, to end the war as an Oberst.

Another successful pilot was Gefreiter Warrelman. Operating from the airfield at Jesau in East Prussia, I(Schwere Jagd)/LG1 was the most successful Zerstörergruppe of the Polish campaign. During the first 11 days of fighting, the Gruppe's pilots obtained 28 confirmed victories and when the campaign ended the number had risen to 30.

Even though he was a mere Gefreiter (corporal), Warrelman became the most successful Bf110 pilot of the campaign: during the first 11 days this young pilot obtained four confirmed victories. His first victory came during the first major air

encounters of World War 2 when Bf110s of his Gruppe escorted Heinkel He111Ps of KG 27 during attacks on Warsaw. During a similar mission, later on, he shot down two Polish fighters over Warsaw within a few minutes. How this came about is recounted by Kriegsberichter Hans Theodor Wagner: 'Within a few minutes Gerfreiter Warrelman brought down two Polish fighters during an aerial combat over Warsaw. His Staffel had taken off to rendezvous with a German bomber unit which it would escort to its target — but first the pilots had the welcome chance to "take into custody" a few locomotives. This airmen's jargon meant a low-level attack against railway installations and the destruction of locomotives. But after that Gefreiter Warrelman waited for his Staffel, near Warsaw, over the area indicated.

'Suddenly he saw three Polish fighters bearing down on him. He climbed steeply, disappearing into the dazzling light of the sun to hide from the attackers. After flying straight and level for a few seconds — during each second he was covering nearly 200m — he turned and then with full power attacked. He surprised the first Pole completely and within seconds the pilot had baled out and was swinging down under his parachute. In the meantime the Gefreiter turned once more to attack the others from out of the sun — again with immediate success. A hail of fire rained down on the second Polish fighter which immediately disappeared downwards with its wings ablaze while the third Polish fighter saved himself by diving away . . . .

'The second Polish pilot had baled out as well and both were oscillating below their parachutes. Gefreiter Warrelman circled around them and waved. Then he turned to fly back to the rendezvous point. "Man, you have done enough" cried his radio operator and clapped him on the shoulder. The Gefreiter must have thought the same because he broke off, flew back and reported two new victories.'

As the last story intimated, the most successful Bf110 unit during the Polish campaign was I (Schwere Jagd)/LG1, the Zerstörergruppe of the Lehrgeschwader, which after the campaign became V/LG1. They scored 30 victories for only a few losses, one of which was the Bf110 flown by Uffz Lindemann and Uffz Radeck. They went missing for five days. Kriegsberichter Hans Theodor Wagner reported at the time: 'Five days and nights had gone by since the two Unteroffiziere — Lindemann and Radeck — hadn't returned from their mission. Then the telephone rang in the operations room of the Zerstörergruppe where Hauptmann Horst Liensberger, the Gruppenkommandeur, was preparing the next day's flights. The two airmen, assumed to be dead, were reporting back for duty and a few hours later they were able to shake hands with their comrades and tell about their adventurous flight across the Polish lines.

'They had run out of luck; a hit from the Polish AA guns had mortally wounded their aircraft. Luckily the controls were still responsive and both pilot and wireless operator were unhurt. They tried to get down as close to the German lines as possible, crash-landing near the edge of a wood. The aircraft was written off in the crash but they didn't have the time to set it on fire because Polish peasants were already running towards them from a nearby village, armed with clubs and accompanied by ferocious looking dogs. The two men threw away their uniform jackets and ran into the sheltered wood. Dressed in sweaters, flying trousers and shoes, they hid themselves in the thickest shrubbery, while the villagers combed the woods; fortunately the flyers remained undiscovered and when night fell they crept away like Indians. They orientated themselves by the stars and covered but a few kilometres each night. The last bar of chocolate had been eaten a long time ago, and they had had to chew leaves and drink water from a swamp. But with unbounded energy they continued to march northwards until at last they heard the thunder of heavy artillery.

'They were caught up in the middle of a battle, but their luck held as Polish batteries and soldiers rushed passed them to the south, not knowing that only a few steps away two German airmen lay in hiding.

'Then they suddenly heard German voices as the soldiers who had just captured the Polish positions passed nearby. They jumped out of their hiding place and identified themselves. Twenty-four hours later the same two airmen took off in another Bf110 for their next flight against the enemy.'

Uffz Lindemann was killed on the same day as his group captain, Hauptmann Liensberger: 27 September 1940, during the Battle of Britain.

17
During the Polish campaign not every Zerstörer returned from a mission unscathed. This Bf110C-1 of an unknown unit barely made it back to base. While the wounded gunner is being removed from the rear of the cockpit, the pilot is standing on the wing, watching the proceedings. *Bundesarchiv*

18
One of the first units equipped with the Bf110, was I/ZG76. The unit saw extensive action over Poland where it gained fame for its ground-attack operations. Some of its favourite targets were trains and other kinds of rolling-stock. Many a train was left burning when the Zerstörer returned home. These actions were the reason why the 1st Staffel of I/ZG76 adopted the white locomotive as their unit emblem. The crew of this Bf110C-2 is getting ready for another mission. Note how difficult it was for the gunner to get into the rear of the cockpit. *Bundesarchiv*

19
Although the scene depicted here took place at a later date, inclusion in this chapter is justified. Until June 1940 V/LG1 was incorporated into I/ZG2, each unit retaining its own codes, as seen in this photograph taken in France in 1940. Bf110C-2, L1+XB, WNr 3560, was flown by Hauptmann Horst Liensberger and belonged to the Stab of V(Z)/LG1, which was shot down on 27 September 1940. The Bf110C-4, 3M+AA, WNr 2116, flown by Oberleutnant Schäfer, belonged to the Gruppenstab of I/ZG2. The aircraft was shot down on 4 September 1940, by Plt Off R. F. T. Doe of No 234 Squadron and force-landed near Mill Hill, Shoreham Downs, Sussex. Schäfer and his gunner Unteroffizier Bendjus were captured unhurt; for them the war was over. *Bundesarchiv*

Over Heligoland Bight

On 19 December 1939 all over Germany the following *Sondermeldung* (special broadcast), was heard over the radio:
'During the afternoon of 18 December the English made a large raid with 44 of their most modern bombers. The enemy formation tried to attack various places along the North Sea coast but were attacked and dispersed by German fighters as they approached the coast. There were many bitter aerial combats over the German Bight. According to the reports received so far 34 English bombers were shot down — and this figure doesn't include aircraft which no doubt didn't survive the trip home. Parts of the shot-down English aircraft have already been washed ashore on the German islands. The crew of two English aircraft were taken prisoner. Only a few English succeeded in breaking through to Wilhelmshaven. They got into concentrated defensive AA fire and were unable to drop their bombs.

'On the German side two aircraft were lost but their crews baled out. The victorious German fighter units which are equipped with Messerschmitt aircraft belong to Jagdgeschwader Schumacher which had already had a striking success on 14 December when it sent the enemy packing by shooting down 10 of the 20 attacking Englishmen.'

20
At 13.23hrs on 18 December 1939, the screen of the Freya radar installation on Wangerooge, suddenly showed a large echo. Leutnant Diehl, commanding LN/Vers Regiment 3, at once notified the airfield of Jever of the sighting but no one believed him — the same would happen to the Americans at Pearl Harbor. It was only after two more sightings by the Freya radar on Heligoland that, around 14.35hrs, the first German planes went into action. The units involved were: Stab/JG1, 10(N)/JG26. II/JG77, I/ZG76 and JGr101. Shown are Bf110C-2s of I/ZG76, on a Norwegian airfield in early summer 1940. The nearest aircraft has the old, and the one in the background the new, type of fuselage Balkenkreuz. Of interest is the silhouette of a Bf110 painted on the left side of the port engine. The aircrew are wearing the lightweight summer flying suit and are being briefed by a Hauptmann, probably the Staffelkapitän. *Bundesarchiv*

Recently Herr Wolfgang Falck gave the author the following short report on this action:

'I was Staffelkapitän of 2/ZG76. On 17 December 1939 we were transferred from the Rhineland to Jever. On the 18th, I and three others flew over the sea for the first time "to get used to it". In the vicinity of the Isle of Texel we got some information over the wireless about approaching RAF bombers in the direction of Wilhelmshaven. We started to climb, direction Heligoland. To the northwest of Heligoland we closed on a Wellington which had already been attacked by a Bf109 Staffel. I shot down the Wellington and hit the engine of a second

21
In 1939, I/ZG76 was stationed at the airfield of Jever (Ostfriesland), near Wilhelmshaven. It was from this airfield that Hauptmann Wolfgang Falck, Staffelkapitän of 2/ZG76, took off to intercept the British bombers on 18 December 1939. During the ensuing battle, Falck gained two victories but was forced to land his crippled aircraft on Wangerooge. He is pictured here in the ready-room at Jever airfield in December 1939. Behind him the unit insignia, the *Marien-Käfer* (Lady-Bug) with the unit victories marked in the left hand corner. *Wolfgang Falck*

22
Drawing of Hauptmann Wolfgang Falck in the cockpit of his Bf110C-2 of 2/ZG76. This drawing by the RLM artist Wolf Willrich shows to advantage one of the reasons why Falck was nicknamed *Die Falke* (the Falcon). Note unit insignia in top left corner. *Wolfgang Falck*

23
On Sunday, 31 March 1940, an exhibition was held in Berlin, showing the Germans various shot-down enemy aircraft. These served as an attraction in gathering funds for the season's relief work. Shown here is the wreck of an unidentified Vickers Wellington Mk 1, shot down on 18 December 1939.

23

one, but my aircraft received many hits too. My right engine suddenly stopped and gasoline streamed out of the wing. It was a wonder that the aircraft did not catch fire because my radio operator, Feldwebel Walz, and I myself had to fight a fire in our own ammunition. The cabin was full of smoke.

'Without any engines, I glided from northwest of Heligoland to the island of Wangerooge where I made a good landing.'

Immediately after Germany had announced that 34 of the 44 RAF bombers had been shot down, the British announced that of the 24 Wellingtons dispatched 12 were lost. Even to this day the controversy rages about the number of participating aircraft and the number that were shot down. But whatever the precise figures, the results of the raid were so disastrous that Wellingtons were barred from approaching the shores of Germany by day and for the next three years large Allied bomber formations did not enter German airspace in daylight. Another result of this air battle was that Wellingtons were fitted with armour plate and self-sealing tanks.

Also noteworthy is the fact that the day after the battle a press conference was held in Berlin during which some of the participating pilots spoke to the German and the international press. The war in the air was still in its infancy and the ensuing escalation would make the idea of a press conference after each air battle ridiculous.

24
On 20 December 1939, some participants of the famous Battle over Heliogoland Bight were present at a press conference at the Kaisershof in Berlin. Many German and foreign journalists attended the meeting. Amongst the speakers were, from left to right: Reichspressechef Dr Otto Dietrich; Oberstleutnant Carl Schumacher, Kommodore of JG1; Oberleutnant Johannes Steinhof, Staffelkapitän of 10(N)/JG26; Hauptmann Wolfgang Falck, Staffelkapitän of 2/ZG76; and Oberleutnant Anton Pointner of JG1. Steinhof rose to the highest ranks in the postwar Luftwaffe after he was badly burned when his Messerschmitt Me262 was shot down at the end of World War 2. This is one of the very few published pictures showing him with his 'original' face.

Flying Cover

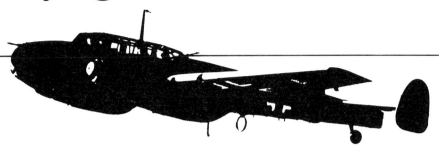

Starting early at dawn on 13 May 1940, 2 Fliegerkorps harassed the rear of the French positions in preparation for the German breakthrough at Sedan. Participating in the attack were the Dornier Do17Z aircraft of I/KG76, led by their Gruppenkommandeur Oberstleutnant Ludwig Schultz. Schultz, a native of Lissa (now Leszno in Poland), was 44 years old and on 7 March 1945 he became the 747th member of the Wehrmacht to the awarded the 'Eichenlaub' (oak leaves) to the Knight's Cross.

Taking off from the airfield of Merzhausen (Taunus) on 13 May 1940, his Gruppe's target was the railway station and the airfield at Hirson, near the Belgian border. His Dorniers were escorted by Bf110 aircraft of II/ZG76 'Haifisch' Geschwader. Schulz wrote this report for the 1941 Luftwaffe Yearbook.

'The skies above us are blue, no cloud to be seen. Below us are woods, then comes the vine-covered Rhine valley, the Moselle carved deep into the forests. Near the Moselle the Bf110s join us. My wireless operator, good old sharp-eyed Stabsfeld-webel H, saw them first. Eight aircraft place themselves behind us in loose formation. Eight more Bf110s fly cover at a higher altitude. They look dangerous, those slim birds, with fuselages like sharks, due to the painting on their noses. "What they get between their teeth, they don't let go . . .".

'While flying towards our objective we maintain a height of 1,000m. Why should we go higher? Our troops have almost reached the River Meuse and from there to our target the remaining 100km is only a small step. The AA from the other side cannot bother us.

'Now the countryside of Southern Belgium rolls below us. Little is to be seen of the fighting that passed this way except, now and then, a destroyed house or a blown up crossroads. Cattle and horses are to be seen on the many meadows. Sometimes a chateau appears behind some groups of old trees. . . .

'Flying a westerly course we cross the River Meuse. A few 2cm shells pester us and my aft gunner cannot stop himself pressing the trigger just to pester them in

25
In the early hours of 13 May 1940, the Dornier Do17Z-2s of I/KG76 took off for a bombing raid on Hirson, France. Nearing the River Moselle, the Do17s were met by their comrades of II/ZG76, flying Bf110C-3s. These would provide the necessary air cover and ward off any French fighter planes trying to attack the bombers.

25

26
The Bf110C-3s of II/ZG76 are easily identified by the sharkmouth painting on the nose-section of the fuselage. This Gruppe, under command of Hauptmann Erich Groth, was the only unit of Zerstörergeschwader 76 whose aircraft carried the emblem.

27
On Laon-Chambry airfield, the alarm has been given. Quickly the engine and radiator covers are being removed from the Morane-Saulnier MS406 fighters. The armament of these fighters consisted of two MAC 7.5mm machine guns in the wings and one engine-mounted Hispano-Suiza HS59 or HS404 cannon, firing through the airscrew hub.

return. We are in high spirits. The security of the Bf110 top cover means that we don't need to worry.

'Now we have reached the point, south of Hirson, from where we will press our attack with the sun on our backs. Our Gruppe veers to the north. The various Staffeln which until now have flown abreast take up their positions one behind the other. The two Bf110 groups following us climb to gain some height and spread out a bit. In the clear air we can make out our target from 20km away. The bomb doors are open and we calculate the falling time of the bombs.

'But where are the French Moranes? Have they seen the Messerschmitts and fled? Or did they have enough yesterday?

' "Enemy fighters below us", the radio operator suddenly cries, "another one, three, five, eight fighters, now they are climbing".

' "I can see them as well", cries Stabsfeldwebel H, "eight of them".

' "Haven't the fighters seen them? No, they haven't damn it."

' "Stay calm, it'll be all right", I said to soothe my excited Stabsfeldwebel.

'And then the Bf110s started moving. Fast as lightning they are heaved around and dive down. Eight falcons attack the enemy, whose formation bursts open, apparently taken aback by the attack. Already a wild dogfight has developed and it's hardly possible to make friend from foe.

' "Now they are at it!"

' "One is burning!"

' "And another!"

'My rear gunner gets tongue-tied as he tries to report the intricacies of the aerial battle. Suddenly there are six smoke columns before us in the blue sky and one aircraft is seen spinning earthwards. Is it a friend? Is it an enemy? We can't make out as the distance has become too great.

'And then we are in front of our target. The aerial combat has lasted only two minutes and by the time our bomb aimer pushes his release button, the cover is back again.'

Oberstleutnant Schultz went on to describe how the railway station and the airfield at Hirson were attacked and how, after the attack, the escorting Bf110s left the Dorniers.

'The Zerstörer now climb above us, waggle their wings and take course towards their home. An hour later and the crews will once again stand on the soft ground of the airstrip . . .

'Even though many of our aircraft came home with hits on their fuselages and wings, every crew came home unscathed. This was because of the protection given by our comrades of the Zerstörergruppe. And already a report of II/ZG76 arrives: eight Moranes shot down during an aerial combat over Hirson. Seven of them on fire. Four aircraft destroyed on the ground. Own losses: none. Good hunting comrades and *Hals und Beinbruch* for the next flight.'

Undoubtedly this report, written for propaganda purposes, is one-sided. On the other hand the French pilots flying the Morane MS406 were very much hampered by their engines which constantly gave trouble as did their armament.

28
Bf110C and D fuselages in various states of assembly are visible in this photograph of Messerschmitt's Augsburg plant. Note their differently shaded aluminium parts. The Bf110D fuselages at right, second row, have their canopies partly installed. The numbers on the forward part of the fuselages, 3520/$_{22}$, 3520/$_{23}$, 3520/$_{24}$ and 3520/$_{25}$ are not the works numbers but the production order numbers. Aircraft 3520/$_{22}$ will thus be the 22nd aircraft of production order 3520, etc. *Bundesarchiv*

29
Close-up view of a still unpainted Messerschmitt Bf110C-4 at Augsburg. The Daimler-Benz DB601A engines are already mounted in the wings. The cockpit canopy is in place and work has started on the completion of the cockpit interior. Of the nose armament only one of the four 7.92mm MG17 machine guns is visible. Note the recess in the upper part of the fuselage, near the gunner's position. When the rearward-firing 7.92mm MG15 machine gun was not in use, the barrel of the weapon was placed in the recess and secured. The trolley on the right contains two compressed-air bottles. *Bundesarchiv*

30
Rear view of the 'Dackelbauch' fuel tank installed beneath a Bf110D-0. Clearly visible are the plywood and aluminium parts. It could carry 1,200 litres of fuel and could not be jettisoned. Soon discarded as unsuccessful, this fuel tank was highly vulnerable and on many occasions exploded with disastrous consequences for the crew and the aircraft. *Bundesarchiv*

31
Brand-new Bf110E-2, WNr ??52 and production order number 3539/₃₂, on its first test flight. Only the Luftwaffe markings and Stammkennzeichen DH+IF are painted on the aircraft which is still in bare metal finish. The line running along the top part of the fuselage is in fact a groove containing a wire. When pulled from inside the cockpit by the wireless-operator/gunner in an emergency, a locking pin retracted and loosened a fuselage panel situated beneath the port horizontal tail surface, to the left of the tailwheel. While the aircraft was still afloat on the surface of the sea, the rubber dinghy stored in the elongated tail section could then be pulled further out of its compartment and inflated. *Werner Streib*

A Country Overrun

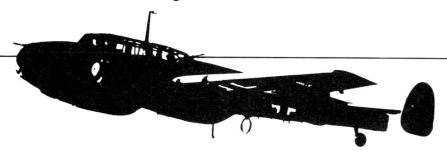

On 10 May 1940 the German Army invaded Holland and Belgium. It quickly advanced through Belgium and France so that the Jäger and Zerstörer units very soon had to leave their airfields in Germany and start operating from recently occupied territory. They operated from airfields that possibly only a few days before had been used by the Belgian Air Force. For example I/ZG1 operated from Nijvel (Nivelles) military airfield or from auxiliary airstrips which had been used during the German attack by the Belgian Air Force. Sometimes the aircraft didn't use a proper strip — just a large meadow. An example of this was Stab/ZG76 and II/ZG76 which operated from a meadow near Dinant.

5/ZG26 left Germany for Belgium nine days after the start of the attack. On 18 May they were at Kaarst in Germany; the next day they transferred to As in Belgium. As (then called Asch) had been used by the German Air Force during World War 1 as an aerial gunnery school. On 20 May 5/ZG26 moved again to the ex-Belgian Air Force airfield near St Truiden, later to become famous as a centre of German night fighter activity.

Commanding 5/ZG26 at that time was Hauptmann Theo Rossiwall who at the end of 1941 published a remarkable book about the history of his Staffel. It is from this extremely rare publication that we take his account of the 5th Staffel's operations from Belgian soil:

'18 May 1940

'At last we have to leave Germany. The Staffel received the order to transfer to As, a small industrial town in eastern Belgium. All flying personnel started for St Truiden, also situated at the other side of the Belgian border, before noon in order to refuel there and so be able to fly on towards Amiens where the Gruppe was tasked with hunting down enemy fighters. But at St Truiden things didn't go smoothly. The fuel tankers arrived very slowly, one by one, and it took a long time to refuel. Our Staffel was the first to finish and because it was already late afternoon and the bomber units had to attack Amiens that day, we were ordered to take-off alone.

'At first everything was fine. Hauptmann d'Elsa led his formation off at medium height amidst scattered cloud. As nothing was going on he decided to see what was happening below the clouds. The Staffel went down through the clouds . . . and found itself in the middle of some 40 Spitfires. While descending through the clouds the pilots couldn't see a thing; then suddenly they were in the middle of a hornet's nest — eight against 40. Who was more surprised, the Tommies or me, is difficult to say!

'Immediately a dogfight took place as everybody let loose and three English aircraft fell away burning; they were all we could see go down in the melée.

'At As airfield the pilots of the other Staffeln were standing around waiting. They had also had a fight above the clouds but had landed a long time ago. The 5th Staffel should have been back by now and there were worries that something could have happened to them. The Kommandeur paced up and down afraid of the fate of his men.

'Then at last a machine with a red painted nose appeared. On its side it wore the Pik-As, the badge of the 5th Staffel. It was Oberfeldwebel Rochel; his aircraft had

32
Generaloberst Albert Kesselring visited the airfield at Bonninghardt am Niederrhein, shortly before the start of the attack against the Low Countries and France, on 10 May 1940. From left to right: Hauptmann Wolfgang Falck, Gruppenkommandeur of I/ZG1; Oberleutnant Wandam, Gruppenatjutant of I/ZG1; Generaloberst Albert Kesselring, Commander of Luftflotte 2; and the Fliegerhorst Kommandant. *Wolfgang Falck*

33
A demolished hangar on the airfield of Nijvel, Belgium. Inside are the remains of Fairey Fox and Gloster Gladiator aircraft.
Wolfgang Falck

34
While stationed at Nijvel airfield, Dr Sierke, medical officer of I/ZG1, found this bicycle in some ruins in the town of Nijvel. This conveyance was known as the 'Penny Farthing' and was first introduced in England, in 1866, by a certain Riverre. It is not known if the good doctor used this means of transportation to visit his patients.
Wolfgang Falck

received a few hits but he and his wireless operator were unhurt and he reported what had happened, excited still by the combat. He said it was the heaviest fighting which he had been through up till now, and he was already well seasoned!

'After some time Oberleutnant Niebuhr also landed with damage to one of his engines and several other places. Slowly the others came in one after the other and by nightfall only three crews were still missing — among them the Staffelkapitän himself. But the men didn't give up hope — the aircraft could have landed at another airfield; they could still come home. When it started to get dark and no telephone call had come in, it slowly dawned upon us that the Staffel had made its first sacrifices. Hauptmann d'Elsa and his wireless operator Unteroffizier Rössler, Feldwebel Schönthier with Unteroffizier Komanns and Leutnant Heckert with Unteroffizier Berger had not returned from the mission against the enemy. Still everybody hoped that they weren't dead — perhaps they had been captured and were unhurt.

'The uncertainty weighed heavily on the men. Up till now they hadn't had to go through very much in this war and what had happened today brought the realities home in a big way. It still hurt even though nobody was to blame. It was a succession of unhappy coincidences: the weather that postponed the take off in the morning; the fuel tankers that didn't arrive on time; the order to take off alone; and the superior numbers of the enemy exactly where the Staffel came through the clouds.

'Six of our comrades had stayed over there and nobody knew what had happened to them: the Staffel wasn't in a

35
After an encounter with British Spitfires north of Dunkirk in May 1940, Wolfgang Falck managed to return to Nijvel airfield with a damaged starboard engine. Groundcrew members are removing the damaged engine from the starboard wing and will replace it with a new one which is just visible in the crate at left. *Wolfgang Falck*

good mood that evening. Hauptmann d'Elsa had led the unit for a long time and trained it . . . his loss hit the men very hard.

'19 May 1940

'This morning Oberleutnant Rossiwall, up until now in command of the 6th Staffel, took over the 5th Staffel — no easy task as none of its aircraft was available for flying. In a few short words he lamented the hard luck of yesterday and exhorted his men not to let their heads hang down but to act with doubled energy.

'As soon as possible the aircraft that were only slightly damaged had been repaired and Oberwerkmeister Cramer had three Bf110s ready by the afternoon. These took off at 15.30hrs. Together with other Staffeln they again had to cover a bomber unit attacking Amiens. Once more there was combat, this time with some 20 French Moranes. But the Kette had no luck: they chased away the fighters but couldn't shoot any down and on the way back flames suddenly erupted from Oberleutnant Neibuhr's aircraft. A short time later two parachutes opened — at least they were able to get out! Worriedly the other crews followed their slow drift downwards towards ground that could still be in enemy hands.

'But our luck had changed and that night everyone was happy to see Oberleutnant Niebuhr — totally unharmed — arrive at the Staffel with his parachute under his arm. He had landed in the middle of a German armoured unit which took care of both himself and also Unteroffizier Theissen — similarly unharmed and on his way home.

'20 May 1940

'The Staffel has been at As for two days. We have found lodgings in some Belgian homes of this industrial town; the officers were lodged in a small hotel. Our accommodation was small and dirty partly because of the proximity of some coal mines. The airfield, formerly constructed by the Belgians as an emergency strip, is a large wide expanse of heath with a few blackberry bushes round it. A layer of fine coal dust covers everything in the village and the adjoining area. Whenever the wind blows or an aircraft takes off it causes a dust storm. We're all as black as miners!

'The advance continues. At 8.00hrs our two serviceable aircraft flew with the Gruppe towards Amiens again and also towards Abbeville. At noon we were told to transfer to another airfield — St Truiden. Most of the men were taken there by lorry straight away. At 15.30hrs three aircraft took off to give cover to a bomber unit attacking Arras. They fought with 8 to 10 Spitfires during the mission but returned safely. After landing they flew to and fro between As and St Truiden moving the rest of the men.

'21 May 1940

'Our new airfield is totally different to the mining area at As — and is made up of several large meadows. The Staffel has been quartered in a former hospital in the middle of an orchard. The weather is lovely and warm. At 14.00hrs the only serviceable machine took off to give cover to a bomber unit attacking Amiens. No fighters were seen but the flak around Lille and Dunkirk was very dense.

'The Tommies seem to be under severe pressure around Dunkirk. The whole area along the coast seems to be on fire. At 17.00hrs the Gruppe took off again and once more only one machine from the

Staffel went with it. No enemy aircraft were seen, only damned flak near Lille and Dunkirk. Perhaps the English and their air force have already retreated across the Channel?

'22 May 1940

'During the night it started raining and clouds hung very low over the airfield. We waited around the whole day but the weather didn't improve. Despite the lack of flying, the engineers worked feverishly to maintain the aircraft.

'23 May 1940

'In the evening the cloud cover broke and we went up to cover the advance of our armoured forces in the Calais-Dunkirk area. The weather was still very poor. . . .

'24 May 1940

'The Staffel again started to pack preparatory to another move, but shortly before leaving it was all called off. At 11.00hrs four aircraft took off and two others at 14.00hrs. The target was once again Dunkirk; you could seen the smoke pall from far away.

'25-29 May 1940

'Again and again missions were flown at targets in the Dunkirk area. We didn't see any fighters but the flak fired away as usual from both land-based batteries and also from the British ships lying in the Channel. It made life very unpleasant! The battle in the Dunkirk area seemed to reach its climax during this period and, ironically, we didn't have to fly many missions: one on the 25th, and the same on the 26th, 28th and 29th. Only on the 27th did we take-off more often — three times. The groundcrew was under heavy pressure to keep serviceable the machines so badly damaged on the 18th.

'30 May 1940

'Early this morning the Staffel's groundcrew were driven in lorries to the new airfield at Vendeville near Lille. They went via Leuven, Brussels and Doornik towards Lille and for the first time the men got an impressive view of the war. They travelled through destroyed villages, over quickly erected emergency bridges, past blown up bridges. Many of the roads were blocked by columns of refugees and the cars continually met columns of prisoners of war . . .'

When the Battle for France was over, the Battle of Britain started and again Bf110s operated from airfields in Belgium. Among others, 7.(F)/Lehrgeschwader 2 flew photographic reconnaissance missions against England with Bf110C-5s, from Grimbergen airfield. Grimbergen, north of Brussels, was an auxiliary airstrip which had been constructed by Belgium's Aéronautique Militaire-Militaire Luchvaart in 1939. Today it is still a general aviation airfield.

But while the Luftwaffe was fighting against the RAF from Belgian soil, Belgian pilots were fighting with the RAF against the Luftwaffe!

Take Plt Off Jacques Philippart: flying a Hurricane I of No 213 Squadron, RAF from Exeter he shot down a Ju88 on 11 August. His big day came on 15 August 1940 when he shot down no less than three Bf110s of ZG76. 15 August was a bad day for the 110. ZG76 lost no less than 19 Zerstörer above England and Erprobungsgruppe 210 six.

On 22 August Philippart, a prewar pilot of the Belgian Air Force, again shot down a Ju88. But then he himself was shot down near Portland at 17.30hrs on 25 August. Philippart was killed but without divulging his name, a Belgian newspaper, *La Libre Belgique* clandestinely published in occupied Belgium, publicised his victories and commented: '. . . Thanks to him and his companions, Belgians help with the fight against the enemy of our country. May he find here the expression of our admiration and our gratitude.'

36
Oberstleutnant Grabmann, Commander of ZG76, and his adjutant Oberleutant Thimmig on the steps of the château between Dinant and Ciney in Belgium which they occupied while their 110s operated from a large meadow in the vicinity.

Shot Down

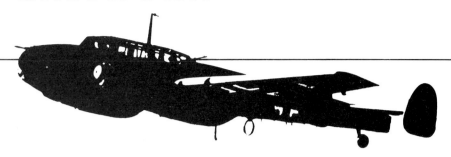

Under the heading 'How they won the Ritterkreuz' the Reichsluftfahrtministerium's magazine *Der Adler* regularly published short accounts on Luftwaffe members who had obtained the Knight's Cross. On 14 September 1940 Oberstleutnant Walter Grabmann obtained this decoration and in its issue for 15 October 1940 *Der Adler* published the following:

'Oberstleutnant Grabmann, who as a member of the Condor Legion obtained six victories, successfully led a Zerstörergruppe during the Polish campaign and took part in the fighting in the west as Kommodore of a Zerstörergeschwader. On 18 May Oberstleutnant Grabmann was shot down west of Douai during an aerial combat and was taken into captivity by the French after baling out. Six days later he was freed by German forces and took back command of his Geschwader which went on to win 500 aerial victories during many missions against England mostly while giving cover to bomber units.'

Grabmann's release from captivity received

37
With a Bf110C-4 of II/ZG76 as a backdrop, the Geschwaderkommodore, Major Grabmann addresses his flying crews at the airfield near Dinant. *Walter Grabmann*

38
On 18 May 1940 Grabmann was shot down by British Hurricanes while escorting a Staffel of KG2's Dornier Do17s. He was able to bale out at a height of 600m and was captured by the French. After spending a week in French captivity, he was rescued by German troops and was flown back to the airstrip near Dinant by a Do17P-1 of a Fernaufklärer-Staffel. After landing at Dinant he smiles at his comrades from the co-pilot's seat.
Walter Grabmann

39
After stepping out of the Dornier,
Major Grabmann is greeted by
fellow officers.
Walter Grabmann

40
At the beginning of the Battle of
Britain ZG76 was transferred
from Luftflotte 3 to Luftflotte 2
and was stationed at bases in the
Caen-Abbeville area. Here
Grabmann is congratulated by
Feldmarschall Milch after he was
awarded the Knight's Cross on
14 September 1940.

41
As we have seen before, the
white locomotive emblem was
carried by Bf110Cs of 1/ZG76; it
also appeared on Bf110Cs of
3/ZG26. However the
combination depicted here is
seldom seen. In front of the
Staffel emblem is another one,
showing a running British lion
being chased by a diving vulture.
It is highly probable that it is a
personal emblem of the crew of
this particular aircraft.

a great deal of attention and it quickly grew
in the Press. Stories about fighting his way
through enemy lines proliferated. About
this Grabmann himself, more than 40 years
later remembers:
'The "fighting back to the German lines" is
a fabrication by the Press. I did not take any
part in creating this legend. The fact is that I
flew a cover mission with six Bf110s for a
Do17 Staffel of KG2 on a low level mission
over France. I got into a fight with 35 British
Hurricanes at a height of 600m, got shot
down and was lucky to be able to save my
life by baling out.

'I was taken prisoner by the French and
locked up for three days in a prison in
Amiens. Then the German troops arrived
and the prisoners fled from the French. I
was freed by a reconnaissance unit and,
after being away from my unit for a week, I
was flown back to its strip near Dinant by a
Do17.'

Walter Grabmann started his flying career in
1931. After serving as a pilot with the
Bayerische Landespolizei (Bavarian State
Police), he joined the Luftwaffe in 1934. As
a fighter pilot he saw action in Spain, as a
Ju88 Gruppenkommandeur. After being
appointed Gruppenkommandeur of
I(Z)/LG1 in late 1939, he saw action during
the Polish campaign. In early 1940 he
became Geschwaderkommodore of ZG76,
saw action over France and Britain, was
transferred to Norway in early 1941 with
Stab/ZG76, and took part in the offensive
against Russia. Later he was appointed
Geschwaderkommodore of Zerstörer-
Schulgeschwader 101 in Memmingen, then
Jagdfliegerführer Holland/Ruhrgebiet and
later on Gruppenkommandeur of 3.Jagd-
division stationed at Deelen/Holland. During the final stages of the war he was
Gruppenkommandeur of 1.Jagddivision in
Berlin.

40

41

Circusses over France

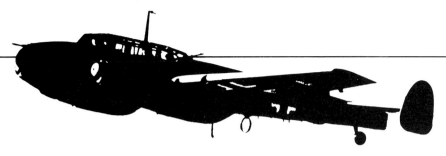

The Bf110 was an effective interceptor of bombers but its capabilities against modern fighters were modest. A defensive measure that Bf110 formations adopted when attacked — the defensive circle — gained the nickname of 'circus' tactics. While some writers have said that these tactics originated during the Battle of Britain, it is quite clear that they had been adopted and practised well before, during the Norwegian campaign and in the aerial battles over France. Indeed, Oberleutnant Hansen, Commander of I/ZG76, wrote a report 'Kurvenkampf über Oslo' about the tactic, saying, 'the Abwehrkreis (defensive circle) which we had practised repeatedly, now got its baptism of fire'.

Charles Gardner, BBC correspondent in France, was a witness of the defensive circle and wrote in his book *AASF* (Hutchinson, 1940):

'On 15 May 1940 there was a fight before breakfast, when a section of Hurricanes ran into 15 Bf110s — of which seven or eight straightaway adopted "circus tactics" — that is, revolving on each other's tails. This was one of the first indications that the 110s were wary of Hurricanes, and preferred to adopt defensive measures, rather than offensive ones. This characteristic of 110 formations still persists — and, when attacked, they almost invariably form the old defensive ring.

'On this occasion the Hurricanes climbed round into one run, and then broke into the German formation, one after the other. Two 110s went down — one without part of its tail, and the other giving out smoke and steam.

'One Hurricane was attacked by four of the Bf110s which were outside the circle — but the pilot fought them off and damaged one seriously. Soon after this fight ended, eight more Bf110s were in a scrap with five Hurricanes and, after a long dogfight, one certain and two probable victories were recorded by us — with no loss to the Hurricanes.

'There were several more fights during the day — mainly with Bf110s, which again did the "circus" trick.'

42

On 10 May 1940 Germany started its attack against the Low Countries and France. Amongst the Luftwaffe units providing aerial cover for the ground forces were the Zerstörer units. These Bf110C-2s of ZG26 'Horst Wessel', are on their way to meet the enemy.

35

43

44

45

43

I/ZG52 was a short-lived Zerstörer unit. Formed out of II/ZG2 early in 1940, this Gruppe operated during the early stages of the war and during the opening stages of the Battle of Britain. On 6 June 1940 it was renamed II/ZG2. Here Bf110D-0 A2+KH, on the left, and a Bf110C-3, both of I/ZG52, are ready for take-off. Note difference in colour scheme between both aircraft.

44

Between missions this Messerschmitt Bf110D-0

(A2+KK of the 2nd Staffel of I/ZG52) is parked in its dispersal. Note that the Balkenkreuze are covered over making the aircraft less conspicuous for prowling enemy fighters. Of interest is the difference in the new colour scheme, compared with A2+KH, seen in the previous photograph. *Bundesarchiv*

45

Parked on an airfield in France in 1940, this Bf110C-4 of I/ZG2 is having its tailwheel repaired. The tail of the aircraft has been lifted by means of hydraulic lifting gear. *Bundesarchiv*

46

47

46

Dramatised impression by Theo Matejko, a Propagandakompanie draughtsman. Shown is the famous escape from Dunkirk by British, Belgian and French troops. This event, known as Operation 'Dynamo', took place between 26 May and 3 June 1940. The ships and the men in their crowded rowing boats are being attacked by Bf110s flying at mast height.

47

A Schwarm of Bf110C-2s of I/LG1 flying over Paris in 1940, after the French armistice. The war in the West was over and the defeat of Britain would surely only take a matter of weeks! It would be a shock for the Luftwaffe when the Battle of Britain started in earnest. Note the very unusual type of camouflage and fuselage Balkenkreuze. The crew of Bf110C-2 L1+LL seen behind L1+KL, Oberleutnant Weckeisser and Gefreiter Brogow, were captured by the British when their aircraft force-landed near Socketts Manor, Oxted, Surrey, on 27 September 1940.

Aircrew over England

Tuesday 13 August 1940 — the much vaunted *Adler Tag* (Eagle Day) — was one of the most significant days of the Battle of Britain. Among the Luftwaffe units taking part was LG1. Eighty Ju88 dive-bombers of LG1's I, II and III Gruppen attacked targets in England, escorted by 30 Bf110s of V Gruppe.

One of the targets was Andover airfield and in one of the escorting Bf110s the gunner's place was taken by a Kriegs-berichter, PK-Mann Julius Gallian, born in Vienna and a member of Luftwaffe Kriegsberichterkompanie (Mot) 7. Here is his report of his flight as it was published in the 15 October 1940 issue of *Luftwelt* magazine:

' " Does your oxygen mask fit well?" asked the Unteroffizier whose place I was taking and who helped me get into my parachute. The engines of the Bf110 were singing their song: an airfield near Andover was to be bombed and we would be escorting the bombers with our fast Zerstörern.

'As we taxied towards the take-off point our pilot, Leutnant M, laughingly called out, "One thing you have to promise me — to shoot first and only then to take photographs! The Tommies are tough ones!" Once again I checked the rear machine guns as the pilot put on full power and we rushed over the airstrip.

'Take-off! Then a steep climb and we took up our position in the formation and set course towards the south coast of England. As we flew we climbed through a gap in the clouds to get more height. In perfect formation the other aircrews flew behind us. We could see the close formation of heavy bombers below. We knew that our leaders had thought of everything: there was nothing in the whole world that could stop our victory. Our Stukas could calmly take their deadly cargo to Herr Churchill. If fighters showed up we would dive down upon them. . .

'Leutnant M called me and pointed at the oxygen mask. I had to put it on now. We were still climbing.

'I searched the sky incessantly. Would they soon come up at us with their brownish camouflage and round cockades? The last few days had seen aerial combats above England like never before. . . .

'Our course to the target airfield took us towards it from the south along the Bristol Channel. We descended through the clouds to take our bearings . . . the flight continued. Clouds made the approach easy until at last we reached our target. It lay below us quietly as we had the advantage

48
Aircrew of a Zerstörer unit preparing for a mission. They are wearing a summer flying suit with, running diagonally, a zip fastener. These flying suits were made of brownish cotton material and worn mainly by bomber and Zerstörer crews. The flying boots are made of box leather or a combination of leather and cloth, and lined with natural lamb skin. They have rubber soles and at the top straps and zip fasteners. The life jackets are of the self-inflating type and mostly worn by fighter and Zerstörer crews.

49
Pilot and wireless-operator/gunner of ZG76 boarding their Bf110C-1. Both crew members are wearing heavy fleece-lined flying suits and flying helmets. Note details of the gunner's parachute harness and the very worn appearance of the aircraft's port wing. The lowest rung of the retractable boarding ladder is in fact a sharp-edged iron. Before boarding their aircraft, the crew had to scrape the soles of their flying boots on it, in this way removing any unwanted mud or dirt sticking to their soles.

50
Another Bf110C-1 belonging to ZG76. In this view the crew are wearing summer flying suits and unlined flying helmets. The pilot is wearing a seat-pack parachute, while the radio-operator/gunner is wearing a back-pack parachute.

of surprise. Everyone was at his post. We flew over the airfield twice and dropped bombs on the large hangars. Then a last left turn to observe the result of our visit. Suddenly all hell broke loose. The gunners had apparently woken up, but the mission was over so we could now fly back. Oberleutnant S would be able to report the destruction of several two-engined bombers at the airfield.

'On the way back we attacked a second airfield. Despite heavier anti-aircraft fire we observed hits on factories and other buildings.'

More eventful was a mission flown by a crew of 5/ZG26. The pilot was Feldwebel Hermann Schönthier and wireless operator Unteroffizier Hermann Rössler. What they went through was recounted by Kriegs-berichter Friedrich Mittler:
'Life or death of an aircrew is decided together. Pilot, observer, wireless operator or gunner, they all undergo the same fate. They stand before the enemy together, they look at death together. And especially

during recent days the crews of our Luftwaffe look into death's eyes very often as they have to destroy the enemy with incessant attacks. . . .

'A Zerstörergeschwader flies high above London. The experienced eyes of the fighter pilots scan the sky. In a Staffel of this Geschwader fly Feldwebel Schönthier and Unteroffizier Rössler. They have been flying together for a long time — first in peace and then in war. During the Battle for France they were captured briefly — they know war in all its aspects.

'Unteroffizier Rössler crouches behind his machine gun and scans the horizon. He focuses on a fast growing dark point in the distance and his jaw suddenly hits the butt of the machine gun. The aircraft suddenly dives and pitches up again. What is happening? He swivels his head about but nothing special is to be seen. Both engines are working normally. It appears that the machine did not receive any hits. What's going on?

'He turns and looks at the pilot: his head is hanging forward as if he's checking the instruments. The aircraft dives again. As fast

as he can the Unteroffizier crawls forward, grips his comrade by the collar, draws him upward. He's unconscious, but still gripping the stick convulsively. His oxygen supply seems to be interrupted. Rössler looks at the rest of the formation — they are already far away. Quickly he grips the stick and rights the aircraft. But how can he bring Feldwebel Schönthier back to consciousness? He sees only two possibilities: either he bales out to be taken prisoner alive, thus leaving the pilot and the aircraft to their fate; or he loosens his own oxygen supply and changes it with the broken down outfit of Feldwebel Schönthier. There's only one option that he'll consider — although it won't be easy to hold the stick and change the oxygen tubes at the same time. But it has to work and it will. Let's hope the British do not see what's going on — the comic movements of this Bf110 are all too revealing. The unconscious pilot's feet are still on the rudder pedals and the aircraft is constantly turning to the right. How to get into the pilot's seat and take over the controls? Following a sudden inspiration he yells at the pilot: "Left rudder!" He's in

luck, the Feldwebel follows the order. He also senses that Rössler is doing something with his oxygen tube and tries to stop him. Rössler slaps the pilot's hand and finally the tubes are changed. It takes only a few seconds — four or five breaths — before he opens his eyes and realises the dangerous situation he's in. Then he turns round and is shocked to see his companion behind him without oxygen mask. But Rössler tells him to join the formation as soon as possible and that he will stand the strain until then.

'The engines now turn at full power and slowly the Bf110 nears the machines of its comrades. Over the wireless the Kommandeur is told what has happened. Immediately the order is given to fly lower and to fly back to base again. Some aircraft were diverted to give them cover until they reached the coast.

'When they get back they shake hands with emotion on the wing of their aircraft. Airmen do not talk very much but through this handshake they said more than any words could have expressed. They had been bonded together in danger and distress.'

51
'A penny for your thoughts'. The pilot of this Bf110C-3, of the 5th Staffel of ZG26, is scanning the sky through the camouflage netting *Bundesarchiv*

52

Bf110C-4, 2N+DM, in an immaculate condition; even the frame numbers, painted on the lower fuselage, are visible. The aircraft belongs to the 4th Staffel of II/ZG1 and is pictured on the airfield of Freiburg im Breisgau. The aircraft, standing on a concrete floor, is trestled for armament adjusting purposes by means of mechanical lifting gear, positioned beneath the wing roots, engines and the special lifting point, situated in the aft fuselage near frame No 15. Beneath the tail wheel is the *Hebelheber*, a hydraulic lifting gear, capable of lifting a weight of 7,500kg to a height between 2.20m and 8.05m
Bundesarchiv

53

Comparing this drawing with the preceding photograph proves that the groundcrew was doing its job almost exactly as the regulations prescribed. The procedure was described in the *Kurzbetrieb- und Rüstanleitung der starren Schusswaffe Bf110B und C* (Short operation and equipment instructions for fixed armament [on] Bf110B and C), issued in November 1938 by the *Technisches Amt* (Technical Service). This procedure is, in short, as follows: After placing wheel chocks in front of and behind the main wheels, a lifting rod is pushed through the lifting point holes, near frame No 15. At each end of this rod, three men are needed to lift the rear fuselage breast-high. A trestle is placed underneath the rear fuselage and the lifting rod is placed on the U-shaped iron. By turning the pivot, the fuselage is raised one metre. Then, two trestles are placed beneath the wingroots. The top of the trestle is fitted into the attachment point situated beneath the wing spar. By turning the pivot of both trestles, the aircraft is lifted until the mainwheels are barely touching the ground. The main landing gear is left extended to prevent the aircraft from canting. To keep the aircraft stable on all axes, additional trestles are placed beneath the engines and supporting beams beneath, and near, the wingtips.
Richard P. Lutz

Maintaining and Repairing the Bf110

52

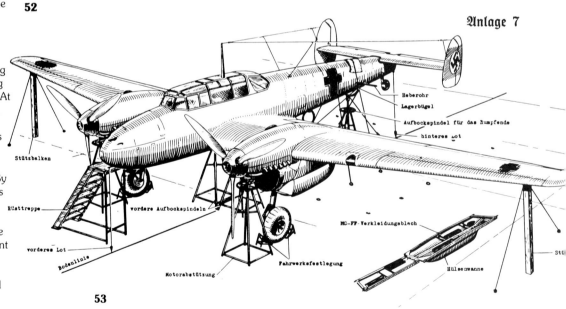

53

BF 110 auf dem Schießstand

54
After returning from a mission, the barrels of the nose-mounted MG17 machine guns are cleaned by the armourers; in the meantime the ammunition containers are being reloaded. This Bf110C-4 has the unit insignia of the 5th Staffel of II/ZG26 and the *Holzschuh* (Wooden shoe) of the II/ZG26 'Holzschuhgruppe' painted on the nose section of the fuselage.

55
A photograph depicting the major overhaul of a Bf110C-4 in one of the Messerschmitt repair facilities. These mechanics are working in far better conditions than some of their colleagues working as groundcrews with Luftwaffe units. The reader-modeller will find many useful details regarding the Daimler Benz DB601A engines. The aircraft has the 57mm armoured windscreen installed.

55

56
Groundcrew at work on a Bf110C-4 of II/ZG76, the famous 'Haifischgruppe'. The aircraft in the background is having its starboard Daimler Benz DB601A engine replaced by a new one. Note the unusual position of the WNr 2159 and victory marking on the nearest aircraft.

57
Armourers at work on the 7.92mm MG17 machine guns of a Bf110C-4 belonging to the 7th Staffel of III/ZG26. The wing root fillet has been removed. Note the hob-nailed shoes of one of the armourers and the frame numbers 2 and 3 on the lower part of the fuselage.

56

57

58

Nose section of a Bf110C before the installation of the four 7.92mm MG17 machine guns. The four compressed air bottles (7a) each contain one litre of compressed air at 2,211lb/sq in; they were used for the loading and firing of each of the four machine guns. The hole visible in the nose (6c), is the opening for the MG ESK 2000, a 16mm film camera. Between the two canvas bags (10a and 10b) — the rear end of the two lower machine guns is placed in the openings — is the MG ESK 2000 plug (6e) fitting into the *Kanselverteilerkasten* (cockpit distributor-box) KVK 17. *Richard P. Lutz*

59

Nose section of a Bf110C after the installation of the four 7.92mm MG17 machine guns. The position of the lower (1 and 4) and the upper (2 and 3) machine guns is clearly shown. To enable the accommodation of the ammunition feed chutes (1a, 2a, 3a and 4a) and the belt link and shell disposal chutes (1b, 2b, 3b and 4b) the machine guns were mounted in a staggered position. In this drawing, the MG ESK 2000 film camera (6) is installed. This camera, containing 15m (2,000 frames) of film was used as a camera gun, recording a picture of the target when the pilot pressed a button on the control column. This enabled the student-pilot to 'fire' at a target without spending precious ammunition. The MG ESK 2000 was also used as a gun camera, enabling the pilot to view the film after returning from a mission and to see for himself if he was successful in hitting his target. *Richard P. Lutz*

60

View of the *Doppellafette mit MG-FF* (twin cannons with MG-FF machine guns), mounted in the cockpit floor of the wireless-operator/gunner's compartment. The compressed-air bottles (6 and 7) are situated at both ends of the gun-carriage. The ammunition drums T60-FF (10), each containing 60 rounds, are installed on the MG-FF machine guns; the handles (4) are used to unfasten the ammunition drums. *Richard P. Lutz*

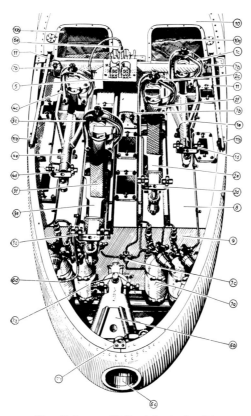

Rumpfspitze, zum Waffeneinbau vorbereitet

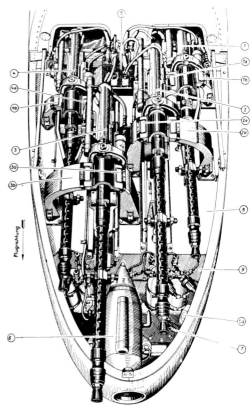

Rumpfspitzeneinbau

60

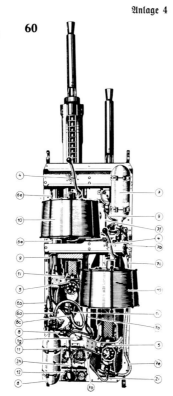

Doppellafette mit MG-FF und Trommeln

61

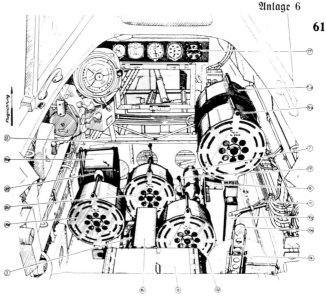

Einbau der MG-FF im Beobachterraum

61

In this view of the Doppellafette mit MG-FF the gun-carriage has been installed in the cockpit floor of the wireless-operator/gunner's compartment. The front end of the gun-carriage was fastened to the strengthened sides of the fuselage bottom cut-out with 12 screws; the rear end was fastened with 15 screws.

The ammunition drums (10c and d) are mounted on the MG-FF cannons. The spare ammunition drums (10a and b) are visible at left and right of the cockpit. The empty drums (14) were stowed at the lower right side of the cockpit. Only four spare drums were taken along on a mission. *Richard P. Lutz*

Flying the Bf110

When the Battle of Britain started, the Luftwaffe's standard fighter, the Messerschmitt Bf109, held few secrets to the RAF. As early as February 1938, the French had had the opportunity to examine thoroughly a Bf109 captured by Republican forces in Spain.

The RAF's turn to do the same came at the end of 1939. On 24 September 1939, Gefreiter Adolf Hasselbach of 3/JGr152, was shot down by Sergent-Chef Combette of Groupement de Chasse GCI/3. His Bf109 came down around 12.50hrs at Niedergailbach. On 3 October the RAF had the occasion to inspect the aircraft and on 22 December it was flown to the A&AEE at Boscombe Down for a more thorough examination.

With the Messerschmitt Bf110 things were different. Early in 1939 the French, as related earlier, almost succeeded in obtaining an intact Bf110. The British had to wait a little longer but 21 July 1940 proved to be their lucky day. On that day, Oberleutnant Friedrich-Karl Runde and his observer/gunner, Feldwebel Baden, took off with their Bf110C-5, 5F+CM (WNr 2177) of *Aufklärungsgruppe* (Reconnaissance Group) 4(F)/14, for a long-range reconnaissance flight over England. In 1980, Runde — now living in Frankfurt/Main — recalled: 'My mission was a long-range reconnaissance flight over England and my assignment was to take photographs from high altitude with our Rb50/30 camera. We took off in the early morning hours from Cherbourg airfield. Over the Continent the weather was fine, with no clouds, but the cloudiness over England made our mission impossible and forced us to return to base. Two hours later, we took off again, but since the sky over England was still cloudy, I decided to make a visual reconnaissance from a height of 2,000m. Our mission completed, I turned to base but before we were able to reach the coast we were attacked by British fighters. I was unable to find cover because, by that time, the sun had dissolved most of the clouds. After both engines had stopped, I was forced to make a belly-landing. We tried to set fire to our aircraft — we even emptied our Very pistol into the fuel tanks — but our efforts were to no avail. We went into captivity — the larger part of it spent in Canada — and returned home in December 1946. I still don't know the name of the place where we made our forced-landing and I would be very glad if someone could tell me.'

62
With the port engine running at full power, this Bf110C-5 is being readied for a short test flight. It was with this type of aircraft that Oberleutnant Karl-Friedrich Runde was forced to land in Britain on 21 July 1940. On this reconnaissance version of the Bf110, the MG-FF 151/20 cannons, mounted on the cockpit floor, were removed and replaced by a Rb50/30 camera. Next to the black spot, beneath the fuselage, is the remotely controlled sliding panel behind which the Rb50/30 camera is installed.

On his return, Oberleutnant Runde had been attacked by three Hurricanes, flown by Flt Lt D. E. Turner, Flg Off C. T. Davis and Plt Off J. S. Wigglesworth of Red Section of No 238 Squadron. At 10.25hrs the Bf110 belly-landed on Goodwood Home Farm near Chichester and the crew was taken prisoner. Their slightly damaged aircraft was transported to the RAE. There it was repaired with parts that had been salvaged from Bf110C-4 2N+EP of the 6th Staffel of II/ZG76. Coincidentally, this aircraft had also been shot down by No 238 Squadron — Green Section — on 11 July and made a forced-landing at Grange Heath near Lulworth at 12.10hrs. On 25 October, 5F+CM, originally built by the Gothaer Waggonfabrik, was airworthy again and the RAE then undertook performance and handling trials.

The results of these handling tests were discussed by Mr M. B. Morgan and Mr R. Smelt of the Royal Aircraft Establishment when they lectured on 'The Aerodynamic Features of German Aircraft' at a meeting of the Royal Aeronautical Society in the lecture hall of the Institution of Mechanical Engineers at Storye's Gate, St James's Park, Westminster, on 9 March 1944. About the Bf110 they said:

'Take-off
The take-off run seems rather long to the pilot, and rudder has to be used coarsely to prevent swinging in the early stages. Optimum flap setting at the weight tested was 20°. At this setting little effort is required to unstick, whereas with flaps up considerable forward force is needed to get the tail up. The initial climb is excellent, and control is adequate during the climb.

'Approach and landing
The best approach speed, flaps and undercarriage down, is about 95mph. On lowering the flaps there is a very large change of attitude. At the beginning of the flap movement the nose comes up, and a large forward stick force is needed to counteract this; towards the end of the flap movement the nose sinks, requiring a slight pull to maintain the speed. The eventual change of trim is small. The flaps take about 7sec to come fully down at 110mph.

'The ailerons (which droop 10° with the flaps) become markedly lighter on putting the flaps down. Rudder and ailerons are unaffected. All three controls are adequate. The longitudinal stability on the glide is exceptionally high. Pilots consider this an excellent feature, since once the aeroplane was trimmed there was little need to watch the ASI closely.

'Stalling speed is reduced from 85mph to 64mph ASI on lowering the flaps. During the approach glide at 95mph the slots are about ¼ open, and this causes slight aileron buffeting.

'View during the approach is excellent, and the landing itself is very straightforward and easy, with none of the tendency for a wing to drop exhibited by the Me109E. Heavy braking can be used during the ground run without fear of lifting the tail.

'Taxying
Ground handling qualities are very satisfactory. The aeroplane is easily controlled by use of the engines or of the brakes, which are operated by toe pedals. View while taxying is excellent.

'Flight on one engine
If one engine suddenly cuts when cruising level at 210mph the nose swings through about 20° before bank starts to develop, the motion being gentle. Ample trim is available for steady flight on one engine hands and feet off, with the dead engine either feathered or windmilling.

'When landing on one engine not more than 20° of flap should be used, otherwise on opening up the good engine to more than 1,600rpm uncontrollable swing and bank results.

' "One control tests", flat turns and sideslips
The aeroplane was trimmed to fly straight and level at 210mph.

'(i) Ailerons fixed central
If ⅔ rudder is quickly applied and then

63
During the Battle of Britain, II/ZG76 operated for a short time from Caen, Guernsey and Abbeville. In this view a Schwarm of Messerschmitt Bf110C-3s is on patrol over one of the Channel Islands in September 1940.

released, the nose swings through about 25° and the appropriate wing falls about 15°. On releasing the rudder it returns to central, the aeroplane does about three oscillations in roll and yaw, and straight and level flight is resumed.

'Fairly good turns can be done in either direction, using the rudder alone. Considerable sideslip occurs during entry and recovery unless the rudder is used very gently, but there is no appreciable sideslip in the steady turn. If the rudder is released in a steady 30° banked turn, bank remains steady.

'(ii) Rudder fixed central
Abrupt displacement of the ailerons causes little opposite yaw. On releasing the ailerons they return to central.

'Excellent banked turns can be done in either direction on ailerons alone with little sideslip.

'(iii) Flat turns
If much more than ¾ rudder is applied the rudder overbalances, possibly due to a stalling of the fin and rudder unit. This is quite marked, the rudder going against its stops, but excessive force is not needed to get it back to central. It would, however, be very unpleasant at higher airspeeds.

'Application of ¾ rudder, the wings being held level by opposite aileron, gives a rate of flat turn of about 150°/min; roughly ¼ opposite aileron is needed. There is a marked nose down pitching moment due to sideslip, needing a fair backward pull on the stick to counteract.

'(iv) Steady sideslip when gliding
In a steady sideslip when gliding at 130mph, flaps and undercarriage up, more than ¾ rudder cannot be applied without overbalance. With ¾ rudder about ¼ opposite aileron is needed to hold the wing down, angle of bank being 35° to port and 20° to starboard. The aeroplane is slightly nose heavy when sideslipping to starboard, but this is not apparent to port. Buffeting of the elevators and rudders accompanies the sideslip. Release of all the controls results in a rapid swing of the nose into the sideslip, the wing stays down, and a steady spiral dive with 45° bank is entered.

'With flaps and undercarriage down at 120mph behaviour is similar, except that there is pronounced nose heaviness in the sideslip. The rudder again over-balances at ¾ travel, while buffeting of the rudder and elevator is somewhat more pronounced.

'Behaviour at the stall
A straight stall with flaps up or down is very mild. Ample stall warning is given by the aileron vibration accompanying opening of the slots, and at lower speeds by the ineffective "feel" of the ailerons over their central range. A wing drops slowly at the stall, and there is no tendency to spin.

'Harmony and "feel" of the controls
'(i) Ailerons
At very slow speeds (80mph flaps down) the ailerons have a poor response over the middle half of their travel, but are effective for larger displacements.

'As speed is increased to 150mph this "dead" region progressively disappears. At 200mph response is excellent, but the stick force is rather heavy. This heaviness increases rapidly with speed, and at 400mph the ailerons are described as "solid".

'The stick force for ¼ aileron was measured at various speeds. The pilot applied ¼ aileron in about half a second, and held it steady. Time to 45° bank was measured by starting a stopwatch when the ailerons were first moved and stopping it as the aeroplane rolled through 45° bank. The following results were obtained:

ASI (mph)	Stick force for ¼ aileron (lb)	Time to 45° bank (sec)
200	26.5	1.3
300	27	2.5
350	46.5	2.9
400	46.5	4.0

'Judged by fighter standards, the aileron performance of the Me110 as indicated by the above figures is extremely bad at high airspeeds.

64
Another view of the same Schwarm seen in the previous photograph. During the winter of 1940/41, the unit was stationed on the German North Sea coast. In May 1941, II/ZG76 took part in the battle for Crete.

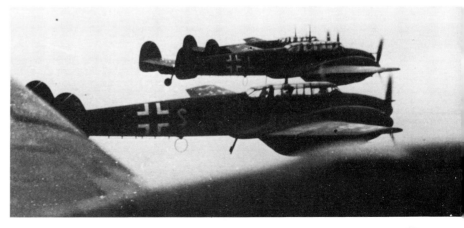

45

Bf110C — Key to Cockpit Illustration. *Drawing by Ian Huntley*

1 Propeller pitch controls.
2 Undercarriage position indicator.
3 Undercarriage up/down control.
4 Machine gun round counter.
5 Compass repeater.
6 Direction finding control panel.
7 Lamp.
8 Machine gun cocking switch.
9 Cannon round counter.
10 Altimeter.
11 Reflector gun sight (with dimmer screen).
12 Turn-and-bank indicator.
13 Artificial horizon.
14 De-icing control.
15 Rate-of-climb indicator.
16 Air speed indicator.
17 Propeller pitch indicator (port).
18 Rev counter (port).
19 Boost pressure (port).
20 Propeller pitch indicator (starboard).
21 Rev counter (starboard).
22 Boost pressure (starboard).
23 Coolant temperature (port).
24 Radiator flap position indicator (port).
25 Electrical distribution box (armament).
26 Fuel contents gauge.
27 Radiator flap control (port and starboard).
28 Coolant temperature (starboard).
29 Radiator flap position indicator (starboard).
30 Oil cooler flap controls.
31 Fuel on/off cocks.
32 Throttle levers.
33 Fuel priming pump levers.
39 Magneto switches (with current isolation switch at left).
35 Undercarriage and flap emergency controls.
36 Air pressure gauge.
37 Flap control switches.
38 Main compass.
39 Oxygen pressure gauge.
40 Lamp.
41 Cockpit lighting selector.
42 Lighting dimmer controls.
43 Engine starting controls.
44 Oxygen on/off.
45 Rudder trimming control.
46 Spark plug cleaning.
47 Fuel tank selector and pump switch.
48 Fuel booster pump control.
49 Rudder pedals.
50 Seat raising control.
51 Control column.
52 Pilot's seat harness.
53 Harness release.
54 Seat lock.
55 Gun control button.
56 Cockpit hood side panel release lever (hinges down).
57 Cockpit hood top panel release lever (hinges at rear).
58 Clear vision panel.

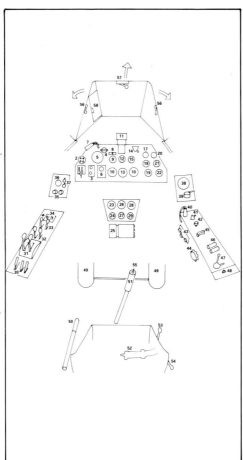

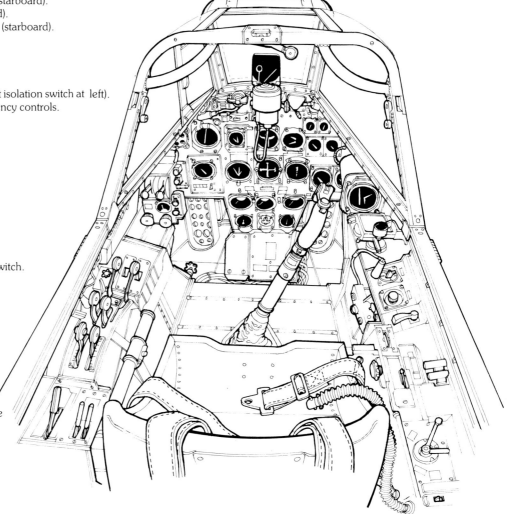

'One other feature may be mentioned. Although when the slots are fully open the ailerons are quite steady, during the opening of the slots, the ailerons snatch. This is a disconcerting feature, particularly in a turn under high "g".

'(ii) Elevator

At 80mph flaps down response is poor for small movements, but adequate for large displacements. The control is heavier than is normal on the approach, but this is quite a good feature. At 150mph response is excellent, although the control is on the heavy side. Above 200mph the elevator hardens up rapidly, and at high air speeds the elevator forces in a pull-out are quite excessive for a fighter.

'(iii) Rudder

As with the other two controls, response for small movements at 80mph is poor, although after $\frac{1}{2}$ travel it noticeably improves. At 150mph response is still poor up to about $\frac{1}{8}$ travel, and the loads are fairly heavy. The dead region disappears at 200mph and above, and response is excellent, although the forces build up rapidly with speed. This is not so objectionable on the rudder, however, and small corrections can still be made at 400mph. The rudder overbalance in a sideslip after more than ¾ rudder has been applied is undesirable at low speeds, and might well lead to accidents at high speeds or when flying on one engine.

'(iv) Harmony
This is spoiled with flaps down by the extreme lightness of the ailerons. At 200mph harmony is good. At higher speeds "feel" is spoilt by excessive heaviness.

'(v) Freedom from friction and backlash
A very experienced pilot remarked that on the ground the freedom from friction and blacklash in all three controls was "extra-ordinarily good, probably the best met up to now on any twin".

'Pilots' Impressions
Pilots' impressions were that the Me110 is a very pleasant and safe aeroplane for normal flying, but that its handling qualities as a military aircraft leave much to be desired, mainly owing to its lack of manoeuvrability at medium and high airspeeds. It may be noted that its wing loading of about 33lb/sq ft, which gives a level turning circle of roughly 1,000ft, would give it an advantage in a slow speed circling dogfight if up against a more heavily loaded twin. Against single engined fighters of about 25lb/sq ft loading, however, it has the advantage neither of turning circle at low airspeeds, nor of manoeuvrability at high airspeeds.

'The under surface of the flap is bulged immediately behind the radiator, probably, as on the Me109, to reduce the exit expansion from the radiator with radiator flap open.

'The tail plane setting is automatically altered — 7½° when the flaps are lowered 50° in order to counteract change of trim. The automatic wing tip slots are very free in action and well fitting when closed.

'The aeroplane was flown light at an all-up weight of 13,200lb. The normal load of the fighter version, at the time of the tests (summer, 1941), was about 13,800lb. At this load top speed is about 340mph at 22,000ft, rate of climb about 2,200ft/min at 5,000ft and 1,500ft/min at 20,000ft while service ceiling (100ft/min) is roughly 33,000ft.

65
This Bf110C-2 belongs to the *Luftdienst* (Air Service), a service that was first introduced shortly after WW1. The emblem of the Luftdienst is visible on the forward fuselage of the aircraft; the colour of the emblem could vary. Several types of aircraft were in use: eg Dornier Do17s, Messerschmitt Bf108s, 109s, 110s, Junkers Ju52/3ms, etc. The duties of the Luftdienst consisted of target towing, supply operations, ice information flights, sea rescue services, communications and other general duties; they operated under the direct control of a Luftflotte. *Bundesarchiv*

A Kriegsberichter's View of the Battle

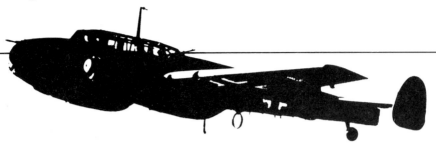

66
When World War 2 started in 1939, there existed four *Luftwaffen-Propagandakompanien* (Lw-PK — Luftwaffe propaganda companies) numbered from 1 to 4, for each of the four Luftflotten. Later, in 1940, their name was changed into *Luftwaffen-Kriegsberichterkompanien* (Lw-KBK — Luftwaffe war reporter companies). Four additional Lw-KBK were established, numbered from 5 to 8. The tasks of a Kriegsberichter were numerous. They had to accompany the Luftwaffe flying units on their missions, visit the Flak, parachute and information units at their bases; interview generals, officers, successful pilots, etc. They operated alone or teamed-up with a sound-effects man when a sound-film had to be made. A Lw-KBK unit sometimes numbered up to 170 men; they had their own vehicles and courier aircraft. Their photographs and films, many of them still existing to this day, give proof of their historical value and the skill of the Kriegsberichter, sometimes working under hazardous conditions. In this view a Kriegsberichter (back to camera) is explaining to some Luftwaffe personnel the workings of his camera.

Benno Wundshammer was a well known Kriegsberichter who flew many times as a Bf110 gunner, among others, during the Battle of Britain. In *Luftwelt* of 1 October 1940 he published the following report under the title *Das war nur eine einzige Staffel* (It was only a single Staffel):
'The 6th Staffel of a German Zerstörer-geschwader has just taken off. The endless rows of appletrees of Britanny and the coast have receded into the mist. For a short time the Channel Islands, Jersey and Guernsey, could be seen, like green expanses with yellow dots. In front of us the English south coast became clearer and clearer against the horizon. The 6th Staffel is only a small part of the enormous formation which is flying towards the north. Brilliant sunshine illuminates the grey-green fuselages of the Stukas; above them the Zerstörer fly large orbits.

'The Hauptmann leads his Staffel as usual. The two Leutnants fly behind him followed by four Feldwebels. It is a closely knit fighting unit, bonded together as if by steel. All of them have already risked their life for their comrades. They all have saved each other's lives during the aerial battles of this war. That is certainly the strongest link possible between men and soldiers. The Stukas fly unfalteringly on their course. This time the target is not a harbour town and the British fighters which had taken off to intercept us now fall behind. The target for today is a large military airfield, one of those from which the British fly their nightly attacks against the civilian population of western Germany.

'Now it lies under us; a large rectangle with, in the upper corner, the hangars and barracks of the Bristols and Blenheims. The

enemy defence has become active and soon the smoke clouds of exploding AA shells dot the sky. The Stukas have taken up their attack formation.Like beads on a long rosary they glide through the thin, broken up clouds.

'In the meantime the Zerstörer fly fighter-cover for the attacking formation, ready to dive down at once towards any climbing enemy fighter formation.

'Now the Stukas attack. The leading aircraft suddenly wings over and dives down steeply, followed by the other rosary beads — an incomparable and wild vision. Like black shadows the German aircraft dive amidst the exploding AA shells. Now the first machine comes out of its dive, the devastating heavy bomb is let loose and rushes on to explode in the middle of a hangar. A vivid flash temporarily blinds the eye, then the hangar explodes like a soap bubble — at first seemingly slowly, then very fast. With a terrible bang pieces of walls, tin roofs, iron girders all fly away from each other. In the middle of it all blue-grey columns of smoke spread out like the tentacles of an octopus. Above the smoke a grey-brown fountain of dirt shoots upwards. The upper half of this fountain is carried away by the wind like a fluttering flag before it collapses in a shower of bits of iron and stone. Now dark blood-red flames come out of the steadily growing grey and sulphur-yellow explosion-cloud. . . .

'All this happened with an unimaginable speed and only now the first dive-bomber has pulled out. For one moment its belly lights up in the sunlight and now the machine climbs back slowly, steadily pursued by the infuriated AA fire. Behind it the other machines now attack. . . Everything is over in a few minutes. The Stukas formate again and fly back, as always accompanied by the Zerstörer.

'On the way back the Zerstörer fly over a town. During the attack against the airfield, barrage balloons have been let up in a half-circle around it and the fat silvery shimmering sausages wobble about far below the German formations. At the same time the English fighters have also risen and some 1,000m below the 6th Staffel the tight formations come up.

'Hauptmann Nacke, the Staffelkapitän gives his last orders to each crew over the wireless. The enemy formation is some 20 aircraft strong and has numerical superiority. The German fighters are ready.

'There — the first surprise. While the eyes of the pilots are still riveted to the circling enemies a single fighter suddenly appears as if from nowhere and flies directly towards the Staffelführer. It is painted grey-green and has a light-blue underbelly. The Staffelführer thinks things over for a moment but that is enough to allow the other machine to get near. Small fires flicker along its wings and already the Staffelkapitän sees the tracers whip by his cockpit . . . But the Staffelkapitän has already reacted. The guns of the Zerstörer fire away and hit the Hurricane at a distance of some 50m just as its pulls up and for a moment shows its vulnerable underside. The bullets strike home and at the same time the Hauptmann sees tracers flashing by his cockpit, flying towards the enemy machine; his wingman has also opened fire with his machine guns.

67
On Monday 12 August 1940, the Luftwaffe mounted a devastating attack against the harbour installations at Portsmouth; I/ZG2 also took part in the raid. Some of its aircraft were shot down while other crews were more lucky and returned home with only superficial damage to their aircraft. Here a Feldwebel, at left, and a Gefreiter look over the damaged horizontal stabiliser of a Bf110C-4, coded 3M+GK; note also damaged flap and aileron of the starboard wing.

68
Flying low above the waves near the French coast, a Bf110C heads for home. By flying so low, the pilot could prevent enemy fighters attacking him from below.

69

High above the scattered clouds, Bf110D-0 3U+AT of III/ZG26 is on its way to the hostile skies over England. It is highly probable that this aircraft was flown by the Staffelkapitän of 9/ZG26, Hauptmann Bord. Note the lengthened rear fuselage, housing a dinghy, and the 57mm bullet-resistant windscreen. Many authors claim that this windscreen was retrofitted on all earlier versions of the Bf110 after being standardised on the Bf110F. This photograph proves them wrong because it was taken on 14 August 1940, as stated beneath the original caption on the back.

Since the Bf110D-0 shown has the armoured windscreen installed, and the production of the Bf110F started in early 1941, these photographs prove that the windscreen was already fitted to the earlier versions of the Bf110, before being standardised on the Bf110F.

'Like a shadow the badly hit Hurricane disappears below the Staffelkapitän's right wing. Its right wing has been torn open and long flames trail from the damaged fuel tanks as the machine plunges down. . . .

'In the meantime the rest of the Staffel is busy with individual fights. Two Bf110s have dived after some Hurricanes, combat is raging and for a moment the Staffelkapitän can still see the Balkenkreuze and the British roundels before the group disappears in the haze. The Staffel has for the moment lost the two machines which are now tangling with the English. Now the iron rule is to stay together. The wireless-operator of the third German aircraft reports to his pilot: "Six enemy machines behind us." The German aircraft turn tightly curve towards the British, and before the circle has been completed, the Oberleutnant has already opened fire. The last of the enemy machines is for a short moment in the lighted cross of his gunsight and he fires away. The enemy is hit. Pieces fly away from the Hurricane's fuselage, the aircraft rears, topples over and goes down in broad circles.

'At the same time the wireless operator of the Oberleutnant's Bf110 opened fire on the first enemy. His machine gun chattered away, pausing only as he changed the ammunition drums. He hit his target at almost the same time his pilot did. Clouds of black smoke billow from the Hurricane's engine and then the aircraft plunges steeply towards the earth. Its straight trail of smoke cuts through the corkscrew-like trail left by the enemy aircraft that had been shot down just before. And the battle rages on unabated. . . .

'The Isle of Wight now lay in front and the Stuka formation was already flying over the Channel, safely covered by the fighters while the 6th Staffel, acting as rearguard, prepared itself for another battle. . . .

'Oberleutnant J suddenly saw a Hurricane on the tail of a German Zerstörer and ready to fire. He dived at the attacker and at the first volley the enemy aircraft exploded. The wreckage whirled down, then a parachute opens and the pilot drifted towards the sea pushed by the steady wind coming from the land. . .

'The German units formated again. The "Sixth" had stood its ground and had obtained six victories — it now had a total of 43 against fighters. The Staffelkapitän got his 8th and 9th victories; Oberleutnant J his 7th and 8th.'

It must be said that this propaganda view of the air war over Britain bears little relation to reality. Indeed the Zerstörer units — and the Luftwaffe as a whole — suffered catastrophic losses during the Battle of Britain, which in the end led to the termination of the daily attacks and the safeguarding of Britain's shores from invasion.

Victor Mölders Recalls

Herr Victor Mölders is a 66-year old architect in the small German town of Warstein. He bears a proud name in fighter pilot circles both for his own prowess and that of his brother — Werner Mölders — who was one of the best known fighter pilots of all time.

Victor and his brother never knew their father, an officer in the reserve who was killed on 3 March 1915. 21-year old Victor followed his father's footsteps into the German Army on 1 April 1935 as a Fahnenjunker with the Pioniere at Königsberg.

In 1936 he went to the *Beobachterschule* (Observers School) at Fassberg but in 1937 he became a Leutnant with the Jagdgeschwader in Jüterborg/Damm. The following year he became a Bf110 pilot in Zerstörergeschwader 121. On 1 September 1939 he was promoted to Oberleutnant and six days later, on 7 December, he obtained his first victory. He was immediately awarded the Iron Cross Second Class, 'a fortnight before my brother got his', as he proudly remembers.

With ZG1 he took part in the operations above Denmark, Norway and France, obtaining a total of eight victories. Then he became a Staffelkapitän in Nachtjagdgeschwader I at Cologne, to be transferred on 20 August 1940 to his brother's Jagdgeschwader JG51, where he became Staffelkapitän of a Jagdbomberstaffel, 2/JG51.

His career as a Bf109 pilot was brief as six weeks later he was shot down during a dive bomber attack against London on 7 October 1940. He was attacked by British fighters while flying Bf109C-4 WNr 4103, block 1+, and came down on Doleham Farm, Guestling at 11.00hrs. He spent the rest of the war as a POW in Canada and was released on 19 November 1946. About his acquaintance with the Bf110 he wrote to the author in 1979:

'My flying training was very thorough and versatile. I had volunteered for the Luftwaffe while being an Oberfähnrich of the Pioniere at the Kriegsschule at Munich. Unfortunately I was not sent to a flying school but instead I arrived at the Beobachterschule at Fassberg in the Lüneburger Heath in autumn 1936. There they tried to mitigate my disappointment by declaring that a pilot is only a helmsman but the observer is the captain and therefore the commander of the aircraft. Anyhow, I

70
Oberleutnant Victor Mölders, a former Bf110 pilot, transferred to JG51 on 20 August 1940. As Staffelkapitän of 2/JG51, he was shot down over southern England on 7 October 1940. Victor Mölders force-landed on Doleham Farm, Guestling, and spent the rest of the war in a POW camp in Canada.

suffered everytime during a dance, whenever a *Mädchen* (young girl) asked me if I flew myself or if I only looked out of the window.

'But as soon as my observer training was finished and I was posted to a Geschwader, I obtained my *Flugzeugführerschein* (pilot's licence) and also the endorsements for blindflying and aerobatics. So it came about that in 1937 I was awarded the "Goldene Flugzeugführer und Beobachterabzeichen" (Golden pilot and observer badge) which some scoffers immediately named the "Weder-Noch-Abzeichen" (neither-nor-badge). Indeed many believed that either one was a good pilot or a good observer, but not the two at the same time.

'Anyway, I felt called upon to become a fighter pilot and so it came about that in 1938 I arrived at the *Jagdfliegerschule* (Flying School) Werneuchen near Berlin. After passing my tests I was posted to Zerstörergeschwader 121 at Jüterbog/Damm, later renamed ZG1. There my job was to convert Bf109 pilots to the Bf110. Now I could use my experience in flying aircraft with two or three engines, in blindflying and in navigation. I also could pass this experience on. The Bf110 felt as if it had been tailored for me. It was faster than any bomber, could stay in the air double the time of the Bf109, and with the help of the wireless operator, one could approach one's target unseen in the clouds. It was heavily armed with its four machine guns and its two cannon, and even if the wireless-operator could do little harm with his sole machine gun, a rearward firing observer gave a pilot a comfortable feeling.

'Of course there were drawbacks to the Bf110: one could not fly it like a Bf109.

One day I was demonstrating to some student how to make Immelmann turns and I got into a spin. I only regained control of the machine after losing some 2,500m of height, and then only after opening up the engines. Therefore I forbade the students practising turns from then on. I helped the next pupil to get strapped in and cautioned him not to take any risks. He was a daredevil and wanted to prove that he could do better than I could. The machine got into a spin, he was unable to get out of it and I watched as he crashed into the ground only a few hundred metres from the take-off area.

'The manoeuvrability and climbing speed of the Bf110 compared badly with the Bf109. Most enemy fighters were also better suited to dogfighting — something proved beyond doubt during the Battle of Britain. Along the Channel front the Bf110 just couldn't be used in daylight, losses were simply too high.

'The Polish fighters were especially difficult to hit due to their manoeuvrability. They let themselves be chased, waited until we were in a position to fire, then executed a half loop, and — while flying upside down — they fired at their pursuer. They were excellent pilots, every one of them a master in aerobatics. My first victory on 7 September 1939 was a bomber and therefore no big accomplishment. I was happy when I saw four parachutes sink down slowly.

'During the campaign in the West, just as in Poland, practically all we did was fly cover missions for bomber and dive-bomber formations. At first we operated from Tuttlingen in the Black Forest and flew border patrols. We were strictly not allowed to cross the French border. It was still

71
Early in 1940 II/ZG2 was redesignated I/ZG52, this unit seeing extensive action during the French Campaign. In June 1940, the unit's designation was changed back to II/ZG2, some months before it was withdrawn from the Battle of Britain in September 1940, in time to prevent its total annihilation. Pictured are Bf110C-4s, coded A2+GL and A2+CL, both of the 3rd Staffel and Bf110D-0s, coded A2+BK and A2+NK, both belonging to the 2nd Staffel of I/ZG52. Note the difference in camouflage schemes on all of the aircraft. *Bundesarchiv*

hoped that England and France would withdraw their declaration of war but, as we all know, this was not the case. When the English landed in Norway the Bf110 was well suited to cover the German Bight and the actions in Norway and Denmark — especially to give cover to the *Luftlande-truppen* (airborne forces). But soon we were retired from the north and stationed at Gelsenkirchen.

'It was from there that on 10 May 1940, and the following days, we flew cover missions for the *Luftlandetruppen* and the *Falschirmjäger* (paratroops). A special experience for me was the attack by German bombers against Mons in Belgium. As my Staffelkapitän, Major Hammes, had been shot down by Polish fighters, I had taken over command of the Staffel. I had assembled the crews and said: "Today we are flying to Mons. The target is the railway station and the tracks. *Angriffshöhe* (attack altitude) is 3,500m, and so on. Well, you know all about it — it's the same Geschwader, the same Angriffshöhe, the same formation and the same cover as with the attack against Deblin in Poland."

'At that I looked around and stammered to a halt: none of the crews that flew against Deblin were there. Even at that early stage of the war I was the only survivor of the 1st Staffel of ZG1. All the others had been shot down, had been lost over the sea or died in accidents.

'In Belgium I stayed a few days in Nijvel. The city looked as if it had died. I saw a group of some 10 or 15 German soldiers, with bottles in their hands, standing on the ruins of a house, having their picture taken while posing as real conquerors. They were from the rear echelon and I was ashamed when I noticed their disgraceful behaviour.

'When the campaign in France was over, I became Staffelkapitän in Nachtjagd-geschwader 1 under Kommandeur Falck while it was stationed in Cologne. As however nothing happened in the sky at night during the summer of 1940, I pressed my brother to get me to the Channel. I converted to the Bf109 and was soon an Oberleutnant and Staffelkapitän of a Jabos-taffel, 2/JG51, only to be shot down on 7 October 1940.'

72
Bf110D-0 of I/ZG52 in its dispersal area on an airfield in France. The 'Dragon' emblem would reappear after World War 2 on Lockheed F-104G Starfighters of the 2nd Staffel of Jagdbombergeschwader JaboG32, stationed at Lechfeld. *Bundesarchiv*

73
Bf110C-4 3M+HK WNr 3622 of I/ZG2. The aircraft was shot down on 2 September 1940 and crashed at Hougham, near Dover. The pilot, Leutnant Schipper, and the wireless-operator/gunner, Gefreiter Schockenhoff, were both captured unhurt. *Bundesarchiv*

Rescued!

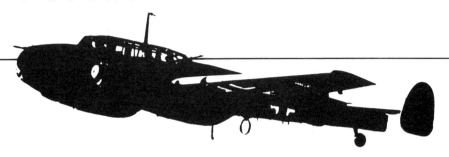

74
During the Battle of Britain, ZG26 was stationed at various airfields in France. This Bf110C-4 of I/ZG26 is undergoing a major overhaul at the airfield of Yvrench, in France. The unit emblem, *Der Ringelpitz*, is partly visible on the left of the nose cover. Mechanics are installing a new Daimler Benz DB601A-1 engine in the starboard wing. Note the tripod, made of wooden poles, the tackle and the makeshift wooden work-bench beneath the wing. *Bundesarchiv*

In 1940 Franz Steigleder from Mainz was 26 years old and a Feldwebel but this lowly rank did not prevent him from being a favourite of Reichsmarschall Hermann Göring. Franz, a pilot with ZG26 'Horst Wessel', was not only awarded the Iron Cross First Class but he also received a large portrait of Göring signed with the words: *Feldwebel Steigleder in Anerkennung besonderer Tapferkeit* (To Feldwebel Steigleder in appreciation of extraordinary bravery). In 1940 this must have been a special honour for any Luftwaffe member and how it came about was told by

Kriegsberichter Fritz Mittler in *Der Adler* for 17 September 1940.

'An airstrip in France: the Zerstörer stand in a wide circle. The Staffelkapitän arrives. Loudly and harshly he commands: "We're going to attack an airfield southwest of Paris at low level. It seems that bombers and fighters are still stationed there."

'Now the aircraft have to live up to their nickname — Zerstörer. Paris is skirted and the attacks made. The crews of the light AA guns look up, totally surprised. Bullets slap into the camouflaged French bombers and fighters. The first attack is made without any defensive fire from the enemy. A second attack goes ahead but by now the airfield defences are ready and fire up at their attackers. They can do no more than hamper the final destruction.

'During the return flight, Feldwebel Steigleder sees a Bf110 trailing smoke. He's been hit! The smoke trail becomes denser and denser, flames flare up and the aircraft has to land near the airfield which has just been attacked. The pilot succeeds in getting his burning machine down. He and his wireless-operator climb out unhurt. As quick as lightning Feldwebel Steigleder makes up his mind and prepares to land and pick them up. But the landing-gear won't come down, an oil line has been cut. He has to let it down by hand.

'The heavy fighter jolts over the ground and stops; the canopy is thrown open and the two comrades are pulled in. But already shots are heard. Rifle and machine gun bullets plough into the ground. Clods of earth fly about. From a nearby copse French soldiers storm towards the machine. They fire, run, fire again. But the German aircraft is already rolling and the wheels are running faster and faster over the meadow.

75

Feldmarschall Herman Göring arriving at the Kroll Opera in Berlin, for a Reichstag session held on 6 October 1939. Since the Reichstag building was heavily damaged by fire on 27 February 1933, the Kroll Opera was used instead for these sessions. Göring is wearing a dark coloured cape; the chain and two clasps are gold coloured. In his hand he holds the special swagger stick made of ivory with gold and platinum fittings; the twisted cord with tassel is black/white/red. Around his neck he is wearing the *Grosskreuz des Eisernen Kreuzes* (Grand Cross to the Iron Cross).

75

76

During an informal visit on 26 November 1940, Göring is having a friendly chat with airmen and groundcrew of ZG26. Behind Göring is Oberstleutnant Joachim-Friedrich Huth, the famous one-legged veteran of World War 1 days.

77

Happy to return safely from a mission over England, the pilot of this Bf110C is about to leave the cockpit. He is wearing an unlined flying helmet, seat-pack parachute and one-piece flying suit.

77

78

78

Armourers at work on a Bf110C-4 of the 8th Staffel of III/ZG26. The aircraft carries the rarely seen emblem of a sad looking fox; the colours are red and yellow. Note the rear-view mirror mounted inside the cockpit. *Bundesarchiv*

Suddenly there's a jolt — the aircraft stuck for a moment as it ran over a plough! Luckily if frees itself instantly.

'The aircraft leaves the ground but it's very heavy on the controls and Feldwebel Steigleder has to use all his strength because it seems as if the elevator has jammed. Luckily it has jammed in such a position that the aircraft can climb slightly. The flight seems to go on forever, and then the engines cut out — the fuel's run out, the tank must have been punctured during the attack.

'The important question now is where the German front line is. It can't be far away — they might already have passed it. They glide as far as possible with both pilots pulling at the stick to land safely.

'They come down in a wheat-field safely quite close to a German artillery position. They have landed 10km behind the front line, with four aboard a two-seater with a jammed elevator. . . .'

In 1942 Fritz Steigleder became a Leutnant and served with the Stab/Erg. Nachtjagd-geschwader 1. His wireless operator during the flight was Unteroffizier Platt. The man who wrote the story, Kriegsberichter Fritz Mittler, also became a Leutnant in 1942 with Kriegsberichter-Kp (mot) 8 but was killed in an accident and buried at the cemetery on the airfield of Dugino, 50km north of Wjasma in Russia.

80

79
Between missions, this Bf110C-4 is in for a major overhaul. The crew of the aircraft are discussing the proceedings with the crew-chief. *Bundesarchiv*

80
Stuck in the mud this Bf110C-4 of I/ZG26 is being pulled out with the aid of many helping hands and a Lanz 'Bulldog' tractor. *Bundesarchiv*

81
Bf110C-4 3U+CS of the 8th Staffel of III/ZG26 on patrol over the French coast. At the end of January 1941 this unit was transferred to Sicily to take part in the offensive against the British forces in the Mediterranean area. The emblem beneath the cockpit is the already mentioned sad looking fox.

81

82
On 15 August 1940 the Luftwaffe mounted one of the heaviest attacks against Fighter Command airfields. Luftflotten 2, 3 and 5 were participating and when the day was over, the Luftwaffe would be minus 76 aircraft. Amongst the Zerstörer units taking part in the attack was the famous ErprGr210. This unit was ordered to attack RAF Kenley, but due to an error, the airfield of Croydon was bombed instead. During this attack, the Gruppenkommandeur, Hauptmann Walter Rubensdörffer, was killed. Several other aircraft of ErprGr210 were shot down and one of them was Bf110D-0B S9+CK, WNr 3341. The aircraft crash-landed near Hawkhurst, in Kent, at 19.10hrs; the pilot, Oberleutnant Habisch, and wireless-operator/gunner, Unteroffizier Elfner, being captured unhurt. On 24 August, the aircraft was exhibited at Hendon, to help raise the sum of £20,000 to buy four fighter planes. *Fox Photos Ltd*

83
On 1 September 1940, four main attacks were mounted against Fighter Command airfields by the Luftwaffe. Not all of the raiders escaped unscathed and Bf110C-2 L1+OH of 14/LG1 was one of the unlucky ones. Attacked by British fighters, the crew, pilot Oberfeldwebel Kobert and wireless-operator/gunner Feldwebel Meining, force-landed with their aircraft on Tarpot Farm, Bilsington, near Ashford. Later in the afternoon, a Junkers Ju88 attempted to bomb the plane and destroy it, but the attempts of the crew of the Ju88 were to no avail.
Fox Photos Ltd

84

Only a mass of burned and twisted metal remains of this Bf110C, M8+DM WNr 3226, of the 4th Staffel of II/ZG76. The aircraft was shot down on 2 September 1940, during another raid on British airfields and crashed on Frith Farm, Billericay, Essex, at 16.40hrs. Both crew members, Oberleutnant Wrede and Unteroffizier Kukawka, were killed on impact.
Fox Photos Ltd

84

85

The heavy attacks against Fighter Command airfields went on and 3 September 1940 was another day of continuous attacks. Amongst the intruders who came down on British soil was Bf110C-4, 3M+HL WNr 2133, of I/ZG2. The aircraft was not shot down by British fighters, but collided with Bf110C-4, 3M+EK WNr 2065, flown by Feldwebel Wagenbrett; 3M+HL crashed at Rye Hill, near Epping, Essex, at 10.50hrs. Oberleutnant Müller was captured unhurt, but his wireless-operator/gunner, Unteroffizier Korn, was killed.
Fox Photos Ltd

85

86

During the night of 10/11 September 1940, the German capital, along with other major cities, received the attentions of RAF Bomber Command. While the British were busy over Germany, the Luftwaffe was submitting London to heavy bombing attacks. The afternoon of the 11th saw the Luftwaffe mounting renewed attacks against London, Portsmouth, Southampton and the southeast. This unfortunate Bf110C-3, U8+HL WNr 1372 of the 3rd Staffel of I/ZG26, was shot down by British fighters and force-landed on Cobham Farm, Charing, at 17.00hrs. The crew, Feldwebel Brinkmann and Unteroffizier Krüsphow, was taken prisoner and had to spend the rest of the war in a prison camp. Of interest are the small white fuselage band, the white locomotive emblem beneath the manufacturer's plate and the crudely whitewashed nose.
South Eastern Newspapers Ltd

86

A Bf110 Pilot in Africa

Thousands of young men died in Bf110s, mostly because of enemy action. But some lost their lives in accidents, like aerial collisions. One of these was Hauptmann Willi Hachfeld, Kommandeur of III/ZG2, who was killed on 2 December 1942 when his Bf110 collided with another Bf110 landing at Bizerta in Tunisia. Six months before him Oberfeldwebel Otto Polenz died when the Bf110 he was flying (3U+BS) was rammed by another Bf110 near Derna in Libya. Polenz's flying career was retraced by his wife in a letter to the author in 1979.

'My husband was born on 14 April 1913 in Osterode, East Prussia, and was interested in flying from the start. He got his gliding certificates in East Prussia and then from 1934 to 1936 he was trained as a pilot in Kitzingen/Main. When his training was over, he and his comrades entered the Luftwaffe as some of the earliest pilots. In 1936 he was stationed with the Richthofen Geschwader at Werl in Westphalia.

'He stayed there until April 1937 when he was posted to a secret address in Berlin. In reality he had joined the Condor Legion and had been sent to Spain. Unfortunately I know little about his time there. But I know that after a few months he had to make an emergency landing and was taken prisoner by the Republican forces.'

What in fact happened was that on 4 December 1937 Feldwebel Polenz had to land his Messerschmitt Bf109B-1, 6-15, on the road between Azaila and Escatron after having exhausted his fuel while escorting Heinkel He51s that were attacking Bujaraloz airfield. His aircraft was later clandestinely evaluated by a French mission (see *Messerschmitt Bf109 at War*, page 36). Subsequently the aircraft was shipped to Russia only to be captured by members of the Azul Legion, the Spanish volunteers

87
Feldwebel Otto Polenz photographed at Werl (Westphalia) in 1937 **before** his departure to Berlin. From there he went by plane to Spain, to join up with the Condor Legion. Behind Polenz is an Auto-Union 'Horch' 830 B1 passenger car. *Luise Leslie*

88
After returning from captivity in Spain, in June 1938 Otto Polenz joined II/ZG26, stationed at that time in Werl, where he flew Bf110s. At the end of 1939, with the rank of Oberfeldwebel, Polenz became a flying instructor at Neubiberg, near Munich. Here he stands in the midst of four of his pupils, in front of a Heinkel He51B-1. *Luise Leslie*

87

88

89

In early 1941, Oberfeldwebel Otto Polenz joined III/ZG26, seeing extensive action with that Gruppe. On 1 June 1942, Polenz (right) and his wireless-operator/gunner, Feldwebel Ernst Hörning (middle), were flying Bf110E-1, 3U+BS, pictured in the background. According to the official statement by the Luftwaffe, he was shot down by Flak, but his comrades are convinced that his aircraft was rammed by a panicking young Leutnant. *Luise Leslie*

90

Airmen of the Italian Regia Aeronautica, visiting the 9th Staffel of III/ZG26 in the Libyan Desert. At left are two Bf110E-2s and on the right two Bf110D-3s. All of the aircraft depicted have Daimler Benz DB601N engines, as can be judged from the white letter N painted on the engine cowlings. Beneath the wings are 900-litre fuel tanks used to increase the operational range of the aircraft. Beneath the second aircraft, on the left, part of the jettisonable oil tank is visible between the D/F loop antenna and the tail fin of the fuel tank.

who fought alongside the Germans against Russia. Polenz's wife, who now lives in Canada, went on:

'My husband was declared dead in Germany until months later we found out through the Russian broadcast "German mothers are you searching for your sons?"'

that he was still alive. In June 1938 he was exchanged with two British officers and returned to Germany.

'He had hardly started his convalescence holiday when he was recalled for a short stay near the Czechoslovakian border from where he returned to Werl. In the meantime he had joined a Zerstörergeschwader (II/ZG26) and flew the Bf110. For a short time after war had been declared he was posted as a flying instructor to Neubiberg near Munich. He loved to instruct and his pupils liked him very much. Early 1941 he joined III/ZG26 which operated with the Afrika Korps. During this time I only saw my husband on two occasions and that for only a short period, when he came to Nuremberg to collect some spare parts.

'In 1942 he was stationed near Derna in Libya and mostly flew cover missions for the aerial supply aircraft but he also flew against Malta. He obtained a few victories during aerial combat until on 1 June 1942 he met his fate and was shot down. At least that was what the Luftwaffe said, but his comrades said that a panicking young Leutnant rammed his aircraft. I don't know to this day what really happened but I have never forgotten him. He was a fine, calm and collected man.'

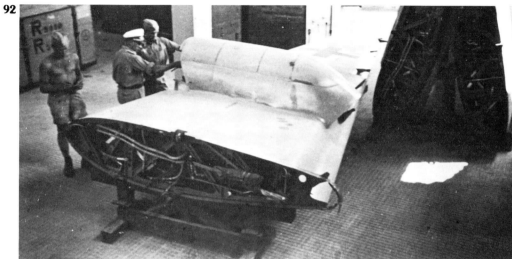

91
The Deutsches Afrika Korps needed a constant flow of supplies. These were brought to the African ports by merchant vessels and flown from the nearest airfield to the troops at the front or supply depots. Shown are Junkers Ju52/3m transport planes, escorted by Bf110D-0 3U+NS of the 8th Staffel of III/ZG26, this aircraft being flown by Leutnant Alfred Wehmeyer.

92
A view inside one of the Luftwaffe supply depots in North Africa. Spare parts were constantly needed and these depots could deliver almost any part needed. Spare engines, still crated, are visible on the left while on the right, Bf110 wings are being readied for shipment to a Zerstörer unit.

93
Derelict Bf110E-1/Trop, coded 3U+GS, WNr 4563, photographed at Fuka (Egypt) airfield on 13 November 1942. Beneath the port wing are the twin ETC50 bomb racks and the individual letter G. Of the four nose-mounted 7.92mm MG17 machine guns, only one is remaining but the armoured windscreen is still in place. In the background are other wrecked Luftwaffe aircraft of which only a Bf109F-2 and Ju88 are identifiable.
Australian War Memorial

No Breakfast for the Hunters

94
Close-up view of the nose section of a Bf110E-1/Trop, coded 5F+SK, of 2.(H)/14(Pz), stationed at Bir el Gabr (Libya), in September 1941. The Staffel, under command of Major Heymer, received its orders from Generalleutnant Erwin Rommel (the famous commander of the Deutsches Afrika Korps) himself. The MG-FF cannon ports and the protective tubes, covering the barrels of the 7.92mm MG17 machine guns, are sealed off to keep the always present sand out. Note the dust filter on the left side of the starboard engine.

In its 5 May 1942 issue, the German magazine *Der Adler* published an account called *Doch kein Jägerfrühstück* — 'No Breakfast for the Hunters' by Unteroffizier Dubrow.

'We were flying a reconnaissance mission over the desert reconnoitring the roads used by the British in their retreat from Cyrenaica, when the observer said, "Fighters in front of us to the right".

'Six Hurricanes passed by us in loose formation. *Donnerwetter!* Six against one, this could be very tricky! They didn't spot us straight away but soon came at us. I told the pilot and prepared my machine gun.

'Then they were on us; our pilot turned towards one and a wild dogfight began. Just as we were getting in a position to fire the noise started. But it wasn't our guns — it was the noise of his slugs hitting us. There was an enormous bang and the cockpit filled with smoke — then the cabin roof flew away — we'd been hit! As soon as the smoke dispersed I saw that I was sitting in the open air. I decided to get out quickly and released my harness. I was just going to jump over the side when I saw that the observer was waiting for the pilot. The Englishman closed in for the next attack. Wedging my feet firmly, I tried to shoot at him. Damnation! My gun wouldn't fire. I armed it again and pulled the trigger — nothing. Had it jammed? Then I noticed a hole as big as my fist in the magazine. No wonder it wouldn't fire, it had been hit. I pulled the magazine out, put another in and immediately started firing. I could see the tracers dancing in front of the attacker who veered away to come in from a different angle. Then I noticed our pilot — his face was bloody and the observer had taken off his own parachute to crawl forward to help him. He seemed to have been badly hit but I had to stop watching because the Hurricane attacked again.

'The wind howled around my ears and my goggles wobbled on my face. But I couldn't take the time to adjust them. I had to fire, reload, fire again. Because of the pilot's injuries our aircraft wasn't taking any evasive action — it was just heading fast and straight towards home. During a lull in the fighting I looked forward again. The observer had put makeshift bandages on the pilot and was holding the stick in one hand to steer the aircraft. It was all very dangerous with the English pilot attacking us again and again. It looked certain that we'd become "breakfast for the hunters".

'But we were lucky, incredibly lucky. God knows if the Hurricane's fuel or its ammunition ran out, or if my firing was well aimed; whatever the reason the Tommy suddenly pulled away and disappeared. I strapped myself in again and tried to find out what was going on but the intercom was mute. At 100m we sped over a group of Englishmen retreating at high speed in the desert. Our pilot was trying not to faint and the observer kept him awake by nudging him. The pilot wanted to make an emergency landing now that we were over our own lines, but the observer kept a tight grip on the stick and kept the aircraft pointing towards our base. Ahead of us awaited a landing by a wounded pilot and an observer who had never before piloted an aircraft!

'The observer turned round and smiled at me. He seemed to be in high spirits. We had reached our base but — as always — accidents always seem to happen in pairs. There was a sandstorm raging over the landing field. I repeatedly fired flares and in the meantime the pilot and the observer joined forces to try to land the aircraft. The pilot held the stick while the observer manipulated the throttle. Then they changed positions. The observer steered while the pilot lowered the flaps.

'We overshot first time but the second attempt worked. A few metres above the field, the observer switched the ignition off, closed down the throttles and then tried to reach his seat again, as quickly as possible.

'I grabbed his belt and he pressed himself against the instruments. Our Zerstörer scraped along the sand: a jolt, a crash, dirt flying — and a perfect belly-landing. We were home again with the result of our reconnaissance.'

When Gerhard Dubrow wrote this story he was 22. Now he is over 60, an architect living in Berlin. In 1938 he volunteered for the Luftwaffe and was trained as a wireless operator. In May 1940 he joined SKG210 which operated from Merville in France. In the summer of 1941 he was posted to Erg Gruppe ZG26 and later went to the *Aufklärerschule* (Reconnaissance School) at Weimar. From 1 August 1941 until 15 October 1942 he served with 2.(H)/14.Pz in Libya and it was there that he lived through the experience which he related in *Der Adler*. In 1943/44 he was at the *Flugzeug-führerschule* A — Klagenfurt (pilot's school) and the Flugzeugführerschule B/C Wiener-Neustadt but ended the war with the 5th Fallschirmjäger-Division Stendal. He was captured and stayed with the US forces in France as a POW until 1 October 1946.

In 1979 he sent the following interesting, even if somewhat belated, prologue to the article which he wrote in 1942:

'In July 1941 my pilot, Uffz Kanold, and I were posted to the 2.(H)14.Pz at Martuba in Libya. The Staffel, led by Major Heymer, was directly subordinated to the Africa Corps HQ and got its mission orders from Rommel himself. Until then the reconnaissance missions had been flown by Henschel Hs126s but when they came into contact with enemy fighters — at that time mostly Hurricanes — they made a good *Jägerfrüh-stück* (hunter's breakfast) because of their low speed and poor armament. This meant that they could be "swallowed whole" with little danger for the enemy.

'Looking for a suitable replacement among types then in production the Bf110 was "discovered" to be an aircraft which had only been able to live up to

95
General view of the same aircraft but here the twin ETC50 bomb racks can be seen beneath the port wing. This view also gives a good impression of the flat and desolate Libyan Desert.

expectations as a long-range fighter early in the war. In the meantime the aircraft had become too slow and portly for a fighter and was only marginally faster than the Ju88 or Do217 with appreciably less load carrying capability when used as a bomber. In the course of the experiments to which this aircraft was subjected throughout the war, it was tried as a *Nahaufklärer* (short distance reconnaissance) aircraft and there was much to be said for it in this role. In the rear cockpit there was ample space to take a third crew member acting as observer. The space normally at the disposal of the wireless operator/gunner with its double seat was large enough.

'The Bf110's speed was more or less comparable with that of a Hurricane and its relatively heavy armament of two cannons, four forward firing machine guns and double machine gun at the back made it a difficult proposition for an attacker.

'Cameras could be easily installed and this, together with the installation of oxygen equipment, made it suitable as a photo-reconnaissance aircraft.

'It was only the numbers of enemy aircraft — usually Spitfires, Tomahawks and Kittyhawks — that made the Bf110 more and more unsuitable, so much so that by 1942 the observers were retrained on the Bf109 which could then fly *bewaffnete Aufklärung* (armed reconnaissance). It was the Bf109 which was then used in this role by the 4.(H)12 until the bitter end of the desert war in the spring of 1943.

'When — at the end of August 1941 — my pilot (Uffz Kanold) and I arrived at Martuba in Libya after ferrying over in a Hs126 via Crete, the war seemed to have dozed off. Our Staffel was only flying two — three at the most — missions every day. We used to take off from Martuba and fly to Bir el Gabr, el Adem or Gazala to get our mission orders from ''Papa Rommel'' and then take off again towards the enemy, usually in the vicinity of Sollum or Sidi Barrani. At the end of each mission we dropped the results of our reconnaissance report at the feet of the *Oberkommandierenden* from the air in a container attached to a smoke cartridge and after four hours at most we were back at our home base. Special occurences: none. Indeed, these missions were so lacking in excitement that quite often ground personnel flew as gunners so that they could become eligible for *Frontflugspanne* (operational flying clasps). Sometimes these pseudo-

96
Inside the cockpit of a Bf110E-1/Trop. This photograph was taken in October 1941 by the gunner, Unteroffizier Gerhard Dubrow. It shows the other crew members: Oberleutnant Genal, observer, and Unteroffizier Walter Kanoldt, the pilot.

97
Obergefreiter Gerhard Dubrow on his way to the local waterhole for a refreshing bath. In the background is the 'airfield' of Martuba, in the Libyan Desert.

98
In January 1942, 2.(H)/14(Pz) was stationed at *Arco Philaenorum*. Returning from a reconnaissance mission the observer, Oberleutnant von Weyrauch, shows the Staffelkapitan where the enemy has been sighted. At left is Kriegsberichter Laubenthal, visiting the unit for the *Wochenschau* (weekly newsreel). In the background is Bf110E-1/Trop 5F+OK. Note the 7.92mm MG81Z Zwilling machine gun taken out of the rear of the cockpit, enabling groundcrew to clean the weapon in a much easier way.

99
Interesting view of the rear cockpit instruments and radio equipment of a Bf110E-1/Trop.

Top row left to right: handle to wind up or down the trailing aerial, turn and bank indicator, altimeter, airspeed indicator, counter indicating the remaining rounds for the fuselage-mounted MG-FF cannons, and the morse key. Beneath the instrument panel are, from left to right: *Bakenanfluggerät (marker beacon receiver), Kurzwellenempfänger* EK (short-wave receiver), *Langwellenempfänger EL (long-wave receiver), Peilscheibe* (direction finder dial), *Kurzwellensender* SK (short-wave transmitter), *Langwellensender* SL (long-waver transmitter) and the *Peilscheibe-empfänger* (direction finder receiver). At the top of the photograph the pilot, Unteroffizier Kanoldt, is just visible.

99

65

100

During a routine flight on
10 January 1942, the crew of
Bf110E-1/Trop, 5F+SK of
2.(H)/14(Pz), had a narrow
escape. Attacked by Sgt
Weightman, the aircraft received
serious damage and the pilot,
Oberleutnant Hantel, was shot
through the left arm. Despite his
wounds, he managed to crash-
land his stricken aircraft on the
airfield of Arco Philaenorum.
Since, at that moment, the *Ghibli*
(desert sand storm) was raging
over the airfield, the cockpit and
nose section of the aircraft were
hastily covered over with a
tarpaulin to keep the sand out.

101

On 17 November 1942, the
airfield of Bizerte (Tunisia)
received the attentions of Allied
bombers. Operation 'Torch',
commenced on 8 November
1942, was in full swing and the
situation of the Luftwaffe, and of
all the other German forces, was
rapidly deteriorating. After the

bombardment, smoke is seen
rising up from burning aircraft
and airfield installations. In the
foreground is a seriously
damaged Bf110E-1 of the
7th Staffel of III/ZG26, while
another Bf110E-1, of the same
unit, is standing unharmed a few
yards further on.

gunners could not even handle a machine
gun decently! We used to get very bitter
about this — especially as when the trained
wireless operator/gunners complained to
the new Staffelkapitän about these irres-
ponsible practices they were ordered to do
work or guard duty. So much for the much
vaunted *Frontgeist* (spirit at the front).

'All this stopped, however, when the
missions became more numerous and
when we started to incur greater losses. This
was particularly the case when Operation
"Crusader" which we called the *Grosser
Orlog* (Big War) started. Part of the Staffel
had been transferred to Bir el Gabr and I
was working at the *Funkstelle* (wireless
office). On 19 November 1941 our *Funk-
offizier* (wireless officer) was flying a mission
himself when he reported over the radio
that English units were marching against
Tobruk, in a sweeping arc near Fort
Maddalena. This report was passed on to
Rommel and confirmed by a JG27 aircraft
which had been sent out specially to
substantiate the report. Over the prior three
days we had witnessed an increased activity
by the RAF: on 16 November there was a
low-level attack by Hurricanes and a
bombing attack by four Bristol Blenheims;
on 17 November there were morning and
afternoon reconnaissance overflights by a

102
The crew of a Bf110. From left to right: Oberleutnant Hantel, pilot; Oberleutnant Genal, observer; and Unteroffizier Dubrow, gunner. Note that Oberleutnant Hantel is wearing the 'Afrika' cuff title, which all members of the Luftwaffe units stationed in Africa, were entitled to wear.

103
A fuel bowser has arrived and the fuel tanks of this Bf110E-3 are being filled. On the underside of the fuselage, between the wing roots, the remote-controlled sliding panel is visible. Behind this panel, the *Reihenbildner* (camera) Rb50/30, was installed, necessitating the removal of the fuselage-mounted MG-FF cannons. The nose-mounted quartet of 7.92mm MG17 machine guns was retained.

Boston; and on 18 November a Blenheim appeared at 10.00 and 15.00hrs. This last aircraft was shot down by our AA. The crew was killed during the ensuing crash and they were buried with full military honours.

'From that moment on things started to liven up. English, Australian and South African aircraft flew continuously above or near our airfield. Our fighters and our Zerstörer could hardly get into the air as they had almost drowned during the last days because of a torrential downpour.

'On 19 November, around 15.30hrs, nine Blenheims attacked our airfield — one of them was shot down by our AA. The crew baled out: two were made prisoners of war but the third died when his parachute failed to open.

'There were no more trips for the doctors, inspectors or mechanics now we were coming to grips with the enemy! Mostly our opponents flew Hurricanes but there were also Curtiss P-40 Hawks. I must confess that at that time I did not know the names of these Curtiss Kittyhawks or Warhawks. When we met enemy fighters which we could not recognise as Hurricanes — we called them *Hurenkähne* — or which did not have the typical oval wings of the Spitfire, we called them Tomahawks or simply: "Curtiss aircraft".

'We had to retreat from Bir el Gabr over Gazala to Martuba. We drove away one night and stayed in Martuba until 16 December 1941. Then the enemy pressure became so strong and our supplies so short that we had to make another "strategic" withdrawal. From 18 December we stayed a few days at Maraua but moved again on the 21st to Agadabia where we witnessed one of the heaviest bombing attacks by the British. Later I learned that British sabotage groups also had their part in the "fireworks" — at the time we believed that the Italians were blowing up their unserviceable aircraft. The next day we made a reconnaissance flight from Magrun and on the way back we spotted a British truck convoy: then we got even for the previous night!

'On the same day we retired to Arco de Fileni (Arco de Philaenorum, an Italian triumphal arch on the border between Tripolitania and the Cyrenaica). From there we flew more missions and as far as I can remember we were not at all downcast even if they had become "hot". We were of the opinion that we were flying an aircraft which could take on any from the other side and only the Curtiss — not even the Spitfire — got any respect from us. We all were around 20 years old, did not suffer from nerves and we endured the hardships of our way of life just as we had done during the manoeuvres of our pre-military training. This slightly excessive self-confidence was proved by the way in which our crew acted when we were attacked on 10 January 1942 by our enemy, Sgt Weightman. Even though we knew that 5F+SK was the lamest duck of our Staffel and that it was the only example whose rear defence did not consist of the then usual double MG81Z machine gun but only the obsolete MG15, we tried to engage the enemy in a dogfight. The enemy pilot got us in his gunsight just as we were on top of a mild Immelmann turn. He badly injured our pilot, Oblt Hantel, in his left arm, shot away the rear canopy and hit the magazine of my machine gun. But now the "disadvantages" of our machine saved us. If we had had the modern MG81Z, the enemy most certainly would have shot through the lefthand side belt feed and this I could not have repaired soon enough to be able to defend ourselves. With the old MG15 and its saddle magazine I was able to start firing again very quickly. Also if we had been flying a more modern machine, then the armoured plate behind the pilot would have reached the cabin roof and Oblt Genal would not have been able to help our "Emil" (pilot) and perhaps we would have become a "hunter's breakfast" after all. Even so to this day I do not know why Sgt Weightman did not continue his attack to deliver the coup de grâce.

'Following this incident I was awarded the Iron Cross First Class and Oblt Genal received the *Deutsche Kreuz in Gold* (German Cross in Gold). He not only saved us from captivity — Oblt Hantel perhaps from death — but he also brought back to Rommel the important results of our reconnaissance and also saved an aircraft from total destruction. We were interviewed by a war correspondent called Laubenthal and Oblt Genal and I got a special leave in Abbazia (today Opadija) to be followed by home leave.

'In June 1942 when the Afrika Korps was once again before Bir Hacheim, the 2.(H)14.Pz was posted to Vienna to recuperate and then to Klagenfurt where the observers, if they were officers, were retrained as Bf109 pilots and then taken over by 4.(H)12. The old Zerstörer crews like myself and Oblt Hantel when he got out of the hospital, were sent back to ZG26. On 15 January 1943 I flew cover for a Junkers Ju52/3M formation and saw Oblt Genal for the last time. A short while later his Bf109 overturned on landing and he died of his wounds.'

104
Oberleutnant Hantel in the cockpit of his BF110G while stationed on Sicily in May 1943. Later on in the war, his unit, III/ZG26, was transferred to the homeland. As a Staffelkapitän, Oberleutnant Hantel was killed in late August of 1943. During an attack on Allied shipping in the North Sea his wingman collided with his aircraft and both planes fell to a watery grave.

Photographs 94-103 are from the Gerhard Dubrow Collection

Over Icarus's Country

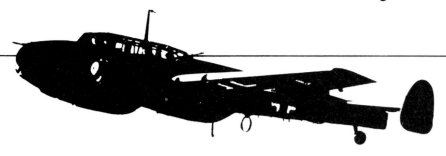

Johannes Kiel was born in 1912 in the north German town of Kiel. In autumn 1939 he became a member of ZG2 and from then on flew Bf110s until he met his fate on 29 January 1944 when he was shot down near Kirchheimbolanden, between Mainz and Kaiserslautern, while flying a Bf110 as Kommandeur of III/ZG76. At the end of 1942 he had published in *Der Adler*, a series of articles titled 'Wir Zerstörer' ('We the Destroyers') relating his experiences on various fronts. This he wrote about the use of Bf110s in Crete:

'Crete was a huge rats' nest of British AA positions. We, the Zerstörer, started the action against Crete. During mission after mission, day after day we flew over and

105
On 20 May 1941 at 07.15hrs in the morning, Operation *Merkur* (Mercury), the invasion of Crete, began. The Stab, I Gruppe and II Gruppe of ZG26, and II Gruppe and III Gruppe of ZG76, participated in the attacks. Although the Zerstörer units were constantly in the air, attacking the British defensive positions, the *Fallschirmjäger* (paratroops) suffered heavy losses. Shown is a BF110E-1 of II/ZG76, powered by two Daimler Benz DB601N engines.

106
During the invasion of Crete, on 20 May 1941, II and III Gruppe of ZG76 also participated in the attack. A Bf110C-4 of the Gruppenstab of III/ZG76 is flying cover for units of the German Navy.

"rearranged" the AA positions first with our bombs and after that at low level with our heavy machine guns and cannon. And then we accompanied our paratroops to the island and protected them from whoever wanted to get at them from the ground or from the air. We flew all over the island mowing down anything that moved: AA guns, artillery positions, tent camps, armoured vehicles, machine gun emplacements . . . .

'In fact we got a very good notice in the American press! An American journalist who wanted to witness the battles on Crete — he had thought that he could get away to Egypt in time — later reported that while the attacks by the German dive bombers could more or less be endured once one got used to them, the low level attacks by the Zerstörer were another thing altogether. He owed his life only to the thick olive groves on the island. There many had clung to the earth without even daring to light a cigarette for fear that the Zerstörer would discover their hiding place and open fire on it.'

107
'. . . We flew over and "rearranged" the AA positions with our bombs and after that made low-level passes with our heavy machine guns and cannon.' Bf110C-4/B, nearest, and Bf110D-0B both with twin ETC500 bomb racks beneath the fuselage. *Bundesarchiv*

108
Bf110E-2/N, M8+LM of the 4th Staffel of II/ZG76, in its dispersal area. Clearly visible are the twin ETC500 bomb racks beneath the fuselage, and the paired ETC50 bomb racks beneath the wings. The white letter N on the engine cowling proves that the aircraft is equipped with Daimler Benz DB601N engines. The 4th Staffel of II/ZG76 operated for some time in Iraq, in support of anti-British insurgent forces.

109
While the I and II Gruppe of ZG26 were engaged in the battle for Crete, III/ZG26 was giving aerial support to Rommel's Deutsches Afrika Korps. Seen here are two BF110D-2/Ns, 3U+CS and 3U+IS, of the 8th Staffel of III/ZG26 on patrol.

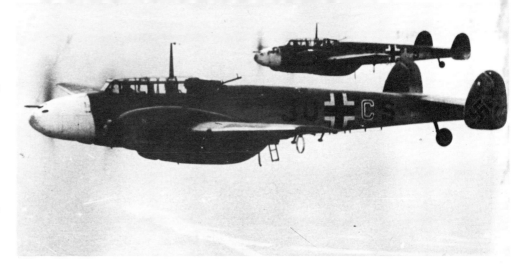

110
Impressive line-up of Bf110C-4s ready for take-off from an Italian airfield. Behind the Bf110s, on the left, is a giant Savoia Marchetti SM82 *Canguro* (Kangaroo) transport plane.

111
A Bf110D-0B of II/ZG26 — stationed near Argos (Greece) during the attack on Crete — is receiving its deadly cargo. Clearly visible is the *Elektrische Trägervorrichtung für Cylinderbomben* (electrically-operated carriers for cylindrical bombs) ETC500. The wording on the bomb rack cover reads: *Verriegelung* (interlocking mechanism) and *Achtung nur hier öffnen* (Attention, open here only). The wording on the extreme right of the cover is illegible. The *Schloss* (lock) has been hooked into the eyelet welded on to the SC500 bomb. The whole contraption is lifted on to the bomb rack by means of a *Bombenheber* (bomb loading trolley), the Schloss staying inside the bomb rack. When the hook, mounted on to the Schloss, retracts out of the eyelet, the bomb drops to earth. This was of course never done while the aircraft was still on the ground! *Bundesarchiv*

71

112

A Schwarm of Bf110D-0Bs of III/ZG26 on patrol over the Mediterranean coast near Benghazi in May 1941. Clearly visible are the white bands around the fuselage and rear of lengthened tail. Beneath the fuselage is the ETC500 bomb rack.   *Willi Wüst*

113

Pilot and wireless-operator/ gunner boarding their Bf110D-0B of III/ZG26. Both men are wearing tropical helmets. The gunner has left his flying boots at home, and has opted for the convenience of sandals, strictly non-regulation footwear for flying crews. *Willi Wüst*

114

Although not of the best quality, this photograph gives the reader a good example of how the desert looked from the air. A small German convoy has made camp on the sandy and rocky surface of this desolate part of the Western Desert near Agedabia. Patrolling overhead is a Bf110D-0B of III/ZG26. *Willi Wüst*

115

Aircraft dump on Gambut airfield, Libya, in December 1941. The aircraft in the foreground, is probably BF110E 2F+GA, WNr 4430, and belongs to the Stabsstaffel of Sturzkampfgeschwader StG3. It was probably used as a squadron hack. Other wrecked Luftwaffe planes are three other Bf110s, a Bf109, a Ju87 and various aircraft parts, engines and bombs. In the centre is the wreck of a Vickers Wellington. *Australian War Memorial*

116

In February 1941, the 1st Staffel of I/NJG3 — V/(Z)LG1 was renamed I/NJG3 on 1 October 1940 — was sent to Sicily to see action in the Mediterranean theatre. The owl and half moon was the unit insignia during the time it was operating as an independent Staffel, under the command of X Fleigerkorps, *Mittelmeer-Raum* (Mediterranean area). Later NJG3 reverted to the well-known 'England-Blitz' emblem, as did the other night fighter units. The aircraft depicted, Bf110C-4 L1+DH of 1/NJG3, is all black except for a few lighter coloured areas on the undercarriage doors and tail unit. This was caused by the use of spare parts from differently painted aircraft.

117

A Bf109E-7/N of 7/JG26 *Schlageter*, in company with Bf110D-3, 3U+FT of III/ZG26 'Horst Wessel'. In the background are Heinkel He111H-4s of II/KG26, known as the *Löwengeschwader*. *Bundesarchiv*

118
A German convoy in the Mediterranean loaded with supplies for Generaloberst Erwin Rommel's troops in February 1942. Bf110E-2 3U+ES of III/ZG26 is patrolling near the convoy, prepared to ward off any attacking enemy plane. Of interest is the very large white fuselage band and the 900-litre fuel tanks beneath the wings. Beneath the fuselage, next to the D/F loop antenna, is *Rüstsatz* B1, a jettisonable 75 litre oil tank.

119
Normally when a wheel change was deemed necessary, sandbags were used as counterweights, to keep the tail down. Here members of the local Arab population are used for this purpose, when a Bf110E-1/Trop is in need of a new port wheel. Beneath the Daimler Benz DB601Aa engine the square oil cooler fairing is very prominent. Next to the port engine is the tropical dust filter and beneath the wings, the twin ETC50 bomb racks.

120
A Rotte of Bf110E-2s of the 9th Staffel of III/ZG26 'Horst Wessel', photographed near the North African coast in February 1942. The unit emblem, with stylised H and W, is on aircraft 3U+NT. This aircraft was flown by Leutnant Alfred Wehmeyer, sometimes accompanied by wireless-operator/gunner, Obergefreiter Willi Wüst. On 1 June 1942, Leutnant Alfred Wehmeyer (at that time Staffelkapitän of the 7th Staffel of III/ZG26) and his wireless-operator/gunner, Unteroffizier Karl-Heinz Biwer, were flying on a mission in Bf110E-2 3U+HR. Severely hit by enemy Flak, the aircraft crashed, killing both men. At the time of his death, Wehmeyer had gained 18 confirmed victories.

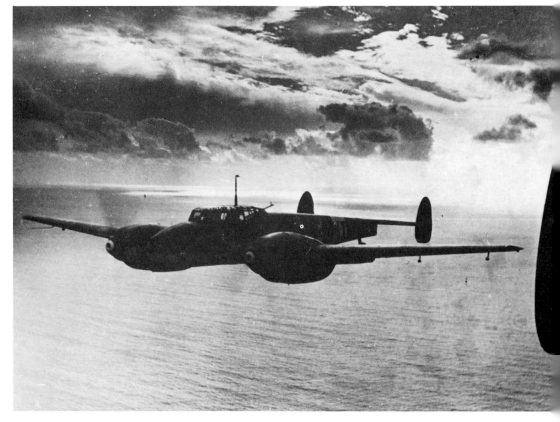

121

121
The task of the *Nahaufklärergruppen* (short-range reconnaissance units) was close co-operation with the German Army command. They had to provide information about enemy movements, strength, position, strongholds, etc. The *Aufklärungs-Staffeln* (F) were attached to Army and Armoured Groups, the *Aufklärungs-Staffeln* (H), to Corps and Armoured Divisions. The *Nahaufklärungsgruppen* had a two-digit designation, eg: 10, 11, 12, 13, 14, 21, etc and the *Fernaufklärungsgruppen* a three-digit designation, eg: 120, 121, 122, 123 and 124. This Bf110E-3/Trop, of 2(H)/14(Pz), is about to have the Rb50/30 camera installed in the rear of the cockpit. To the left of the groundcrew member on the wing, the flare chute opening is visible. The position of this chute was sometimes situated beneath the middle part of the cockpit. The stencil marking, beneath the first-aid kit panel, reads: *Einsteigleiter, Knopf drücken* (Boarding ladder, press button). Near the trailing edge of the wing is the red and white coloured indicator rod for the coolant radiator, indicating to the pilot the position of the exit flaps. *Bundesarchiv*

122
This peaceful scene in the African desert makes one forget that there is a war going on. The parked Bf110E-1s have their engines, forward fuselage and cockpit, covered with tarpaulins and blankets to protect these vital parts against the sand and the glaring sun.

122

123

123
Bf110E-1/Trop 3U+MR of 7/ZG26 flying over a heavily bombed area of the African desert. On the coolant radiator side the marking: 50% Glykol, is visible. Beneath the letter R there is a very interesting feature — an additional, jettisonable, armoured oil tank, Rüstsatz B1, containing 75 litres of lubricant oil. The oil could be pumped manually into the two 35-litre oil tanks situated in the wings, behind the engines. The pump and change-over switch were installed in the rear of the cockpit. This Rüstsatz B1 was sometimes mounted on long-range reconnaissance Bf110s, together with Rüstsatz B2 — two jettisonable 300 or 900 litre fuel tanks, mounted beneath the wings. Note that the wartime censor has 'removed' the attachment points for these fuel tanks.

Accidents Did Happen

In wartime, while many aircraft are lost due to enemy action, it is amazing just how many are involved in accidents. During the year 1941 the Luftwaffe noted more than 120 accidents involving Bf110 aircraft. They were as follows:

Left-hand column (casualties)
Nil=No injuries
L=Slightly injured
S=Seriously injured
T=Killed (*Tot*)

Right-hand column (damage to aircraft)
L=Slight damage
S=Serious damage
V=Destroyed (*Vernichtet*)

Markings	Cause of Accident	Casualties				Damage to Aircraft		
		Nil	L	S	T	L	S	V
January								
3U+KM	Crashed during formation flight (4/ZG26)				2			√
G9+AT	Engine trouble during high altitude flight, belly landed (9/ZG1)			2		√		
MS+FN	Engine fire, landed on water, rescued from dinghy after 8½ hours (5/ZG76)	1		1				√
U8+LH	Crashed overshooting on one engine (1/ZG26)		1		1	√		
February								
2N+HM	Hit ground on mountain slope (4/ZG76)				2			
G9+BL	Hit by Flak, crew baled out, one parachute failed to open (3/ZG1)	1			1			
G9+BN	Tyre burst on take-off, overturned (5/ZG1)				1	√		
G9+FP	Lost bearings due to engine and radio failure, landed in wood (6/ZG1)		2					√
L1+AL	Skidded gliding in (3/LG1)				1			√
DD+HM	Trouble during single-engined flight, landed in wood, overturned	1			1			√
4U+XK	No witnesses. Accident happened abroad (2 (F)/123)				2			√
March								
??+??	No witnesses to accident				2			√
G9+BD	Skidded in bank (Stab III/ZG1)				2			√
G9+ER	Forced landing after being shot up (7/ZG1)	1	1					√

Markings	Cause of Accident	Casualties				Damage to Aircraft		
		Nil	*L*	*S*	*T*	*L*	*S*	*V*
LI+AL	Fault on adjusting drive of left airscrew, crashed shortly after take-off (3/LG1)				2			√
M8+YE	Engine trouble on take-off, crashed on the airfield perimeter (Stab IV/ZG76)	2					√	
A2+BH	Collided during formation flight with Bf110C U8+LL (1/ZG2)				2			√
CI+NR	Stalled after lifting off	1	1				√	
U8+LL	Collided during formation flight with Bf110C A2+BH (3/ZG26)				2			√
M8+AM or QM	Crashed during training aerobatic flight (4/ZG16)				2			√
M8+IN	Forced landing during navigational flight, overturned (5/ZG76)		2				√	

April

Markings	Cause of Accident	Casualties				Damage to Aircraft		
3U+ER	Crashed in a sandstorm (7/ZG26)				3			√
G9+EN	Crashed in the sea, reason unknown (5/ZG1)				2			√
G9+LM	Engine trouble due to failure of the fuel pump supply system, crash landed, overturned (4/ZG1)			2				√
G9+MM	Caught fire in the air (4/ZG1)				2			√
PC+ZR	Engine trouble, crashed				2			√
5D+FL	Pilot error, tipped on nose (3(F)/31)	1						√

May

Markings	Cause of Accident	Casualties				Damage to Aircraft		
2N+CP	Oleo leg broke, overturned (6/ZG76)			1	2	√		
3U+AS	Crashed in the sea. Crew not found (8/ZG26)				2		√	
A2+NL	Crashed before landing, reason not established (3/ZG2)				2		√	

124
Anybody home? This Bf110C ran out of runway on the airfield of Wevelgem, Belgium, and crashed into a hangar.
Ewald Delbaere

Markings	Cause of Accident	Casualties				Damage to Aircraft		
		Nil	L	S	T	L	S	V
G9+EU	Fire in cockpit, force landed at night (10/ZG1)		1		1			√
G9+FU	Crashed during night circuit of airfield (10/ZG1)				2			√
G9+KN	Shot up by enemy, belly landed (5/ZG1)		2			√		
L1+BL	Collision during an air battle, baled out at high speeds (3/LG1)		1		1			√
M8+DE	Caught in obstruction during take-off (Stab IV/ZG76)	No details						
M8+NN	Shot up by enemy, engine failure (5/ZG76)	2					√	
SE+AE	Aircraft in spin, crew baled out too late				2			√
G9+GM	Failure of artificial horizon during a night flight, crashed in flames. One crew member baled out (?/ZG1)	1			1			√
KE+YN	During bomb dropping at extremely low level, tail unit hit by bomb rebounding, crashed in sea. One crew member not recovered				2		√	

June

Markings	Cause of Accident	Nil	L	S	T	L	S	V
2N+KT	Scrambled with following wind, undercarriage collapsed on airfield perimeter (9/ZG76)	1			1	√		
2N+XT	Hard landing, tipped on left wing (9/ZG76)	1			1			√
BB+UN	Undercarriage fault, belly landed		1			√		
F6+NO	Engine trouble after take-off, crash landed ((F)/122)				1			√
G9+AM	Radio failure, fuel shortage, hard landing (4/ZG1)	1			1	√		
G9+BN	Engine failure during night fighting, crashed from 200m (5/ZG1)				2			√
G9+CU	Crashed shortly after night take-off (10/ZG1)				2			√
H8+EM	Fuel shortage during night flight, force landed, overturned (4(H)/33)	2			1			√
KJ+ZO	Crashed in turn with lowered landing flaps, one engine dead, overturned				2			√
M8+JH	Fuel trouble, force landed in sea. One drowned (1/ZG76)	1			1			√

125
This landing was not very successful because the aircraft overturned in the process. The aircraft, Bf110D-3 3U+BD, WNr 3873 belonging to the Gruppenstabstaffel of III/ZG26, is in for very extensive repairs. The black areas, near the underwing Balkenkreuz, mark the place where the ETC50 bomb racks are to be installed. *Bundesarchiv*

Markings	Cause of Accident	Casualties				Damage to Aircraft		
		Nil	L	S	T	L	S	V
M8+WP	Spun after banking on overshoot with lowered undercarriage and landing flaps (6/ZG76)				2		√	
0 3179	Crashed due to enemy fire, exploded				2			√
S9+KM	Tyre burst when touching down (4/EGr210)	3					√	
S9+LK	Single-engined landing, crashed (2/EGr210)	1	1					√
S9+LL	Undercarriage collapsed when taxying (3/EGr210)	1	1			√		
SI+ZG	Crashed after take-off, one engine stopped				1		√	
VC+DR	Low level attack on passenger train. Hit train				1			√
LI+MK	Engine trouble on take-off, crashed			1			√	
SE+ZS	Crashed when overshooting			1			√	
S9+EL	Did not pull out of practice dive (3/EGr210)				2			√
3U+GP	Undercarriage trouble after take-off. Stalled when force landing. Overturned (6/ZG26)	1			1		√	

126
A Bf110E-0 photographed after a crash landing in the African desert. It seems that the starboard engine caught fire, forcing the pilot to land as quickly as possible. The unit code, 4F+?K, remains a mystery. *Bundesarchiv*

127
'Look what you've done, you naughty boy!' The pilot of this Bf110E-1/Trop, 5F+PK, of AufklGr14, received a lot of attention after managing to land his stricken aircraft on the rocky soil of the desert. The wind, playing in the shirts of the bystanders, makes them look like hunch-backs! *Bundesarchiv*

128
Bf110E S9+EM belonging to
SKG210, standing on its nose,
showing us a very interesting
feature. Beneath both wings are
two paired *Roste* (Grids)
24 SD2/XII. Each grid carried 12
Schlachtfliegerbomben SD2
(anti-personnel bombs), which
were used in the anti-partisan
warfare, in Russia.
Bundesarchiv

129
After being damaged by a British
night fighter, this Bf110F-2 pilot
had no other option than to crash
land. Salvage crews are using
inflatable bags and lifting jacks to
raise the aircraft and to put it
back on its undercarriage.
Bundesarchiv

Markings	Cause of Accident	Casualties				Damage to Aircraft		
		Nil	L	S	T	L	S	V
July								
3U+KF	Engine trouble after take-off, hit cable and crashed (Stab V/ZG26)		2	1				√
DK+ZZ	Started by mechanic, crashed shortly after take-off				1			√
G9+HS	Trouble with both engines, hit tree (8/NJG1)			1	1	√		
G9+LR	Engine trouble, belly landed (7/NJG1)		2			√		
LJ+BK	Lost bearings in fog. Flew into mountain				2			√
MA+FY	Overshot at too low a speed			1		√		
M8+FM	Touched down too late and overturned (4/ZG76)			1	1	√		
TG+LA	Engine trouble at take-off, crashed				1			√
M8+VE	Hit a mast during convoy escort, crashed in the sea (Stab IV/ZG76)				2			√
SF+YZ	Crashed in dive				2			√
August								
6M+HL	Faults in the oxygen supply system ((F)/11)	2	1					
DK+L1	Crashed during night cross-country flight				2			√
G9+KP	Hit ground overshooting (6/NJG1)				2			√
GF+WK	Landed too late in bank, undercarriage sheared off	2				√		
KB+UJ	Engine trouble after take-off, stalled, overturned		1	1				√
KC+RY	Crashed during night training flight				2			√
SD+ZY	Collided changing position in formation				2			√
2N+LT	Engine trouble banking. Crashed in turn (9/ZG76)		1		1			√
5F+RK	Engine failed, crash landed (2/(H)14)	2				√		
September								
CJ+NS	Spun in during steep turn	1			1			√
G9+IU	Crashed during night flight (10/NJG1)				2			√
G9+MU	Crashed during night flight (10/NJG1)				2			√
H8+CM	Collided in mid air (probably misprint for *M8*)				3			√
L1+EK	Steep turn with undercarriage and flaps powered. Crashed in flames (LG1)		2					√
TG+FP	Crashed during training dive				2			√
TI+ZL	Hit ground with wing whilst landing and overturned	2		1				√
VC+EQ	Crashed during high altitude night flight				2			√
2N+YT	Crashed during night circuit of airfield (9/ZG76)				2			√
TD+GP	Signal flares fired in aircraft during night flight. Aircraft caught fire, crew baled out. One uninjured, one slighlty injured							√
VC+ES	Engine damage during circuit, crash landed		1	1		√		
BC+HE	Flew into wooded hillside in the night				2		√	
CE+CL	Engine trouble, crashed vertically after overshoot				2		√	
October								
3U+HR	Forced landing (7/ZG26)		3			√		
3U+MW	Hit water during shooting and ditched (12/ZG76)	2					√	
6M+AL	Tyre burst landing, stood on nose ((F)11)	3					√	
6M+IL	Crash landed in bad terrain ((F)11)	2	1			√		
BC+FU	Crash landed during ferry flight			1				√
CS+NB	Engine trouble after take-off, crashed vertically				1			√
DC+AH	Crashed on touchdown after night training flight and burst into flames				2			√
G9+ET	Hit ground during 'searchlight flight' (9/NJG1)				2			√

Markings	Cause of Accident	Casualties				Damage to Aircraft		
		Nil	*L*	*S*	*T*	*L*	*S*	*V*
KF+PH	Crashed banking in fog				2			✓
TD+KB	Landed on one engine, overturned		1		1	✓		
VK+GK	Accident without cause determined				2			✓
WNr 3554	Crashed and caught fire during night training				2			✓
TB+CK	Dazzled by searchlight(s)				2			✓
November								
D5+AN	Crashed during night fighter training (5/NJG3)				2			✓
D5+FH	Crashed due to icing (1/NJG3)				2			✓
M8+IM	Crashed in flames, crew baled out (4/ZG76)	1	1		1			✓
PH+IT	Crashed landing at dusk				1	✓		
SF+UD	Crashed during night circuit of airfield				1		✓	
TF+CQ	Controls damaged, crew baled out			2			✓	
VN+CS	Engine failed, spun in				1		✓	
NG+XM	Pilot taken ill, had not eaten breakfast, observer baled out		1		1		✓	
BM 3119	Crashed during night training flight				2		✓	
December								
BA+OD	Crashed in stall				2		✓	
BD+WF	Crashed during night flight				2		✓	
BO+AG	Crashed during forced landing at night				2		✓	
G9+BM	Crashed during night flight (4/NJG1)				2		✓	
KC+UD	Controls jammed, engine trouble, crew baled out. One killed after hitting wings		1		1			✓
VB+HT	Taxied into ditch	1	1			✓		
B5+B7*	Crashed in a steep turn after night training				2		✓	
M8+HN	Crashed after pilot dazzled by searchlight beams (4/ZG76)				2		✓	
S9+GL	Crashed during training (SKG210)				2			✓

*B5 not identified in 1941, but used by Stab FA Gr3 20/8/44

130
The most famous crash of them all! On 10 May 1941, Rudolf Hess made his dramatic flight from Germany to Scotland. Flying a highly modified Bf110D-3, VJ+OQ WNr 3869, he took off from Augsburg airfield at 17.45hrs and came down by parachute near the small village of Eaglesham, southwest of Glasgow, around 23.00hrs. His aircraft crashed at 23.09hrs near Bonyton Moor, southwest of Glasgow. The fuselage aft of the wing trailing edge is in the custody of the Imperial War Museum.
Australian War Memorial

Operation 'Barbarossa'

Hauptmann Theo Rossiwall, Staffelkapitän of 5/ZG26 wrote the following description of his first mission against Russia:

'Early on 22 June all hell broke loose. Here in the east the sun rises damned early — so take-off had been ordered for 0250hrs. The groundcrew had to be at the aircraft at 0030hrs. At exactly 3 o'clock the battle on the ground started. For the Staffel, clawing for height above the airfield, it was a fantastic sight. In the quiet and the dark of the morning suddenly fire spouted from thousands and thousands of barrels of every calibre creating a glowing snake below us on the awakening countryside. On the other side of the border one could see the points of impact. A hurricane had burst loose on the Bolshevik troops standing at the ready . . . '

Hauptmann Johannes Kiel saw it like this:
'I will never forget 22 June 1941. We took off while it was still dark and below us the dark earth lay in a deep sleep. When we crossed the border I looked at the luminous dial of the clock. Suddenly, at the prearranged time, the German batteries opened fire. As far as one could see from north to south it was as if the earth was torn open by forces below the ground. Coloured bloody red, the sun slowly rose through the far away mists . . . .

'The Soviet aircraft stood on their airfield lined up as if on parade, ready to take-off. We dived down upon them, dropped our bombs and then began firing away with our machine guns. We only stopped when we could see fires everywhere. Forty to fifty aircraft were destroyed on one airfield, their hangars demolished and the runway cratered. As we didn't have any bombs left

after this attack, we flew to another airfield right down on the deck and attacked with our guns. There too, the aircraft were lined up perfectly — in only a few minutes black clouds of smoke rose upwards . . . .

'But this was only the beginning. From then on the Russians defended their airfields with AA artillery. For us that meant that we had to prepare every attack very carefully. Each of us had a specific task. For example, we had to attack one airfield where some 50 aircraft of all kinds were supposed to be stationed. Before the attack there was a detailed briefing using aerial photographs which had been taken by one of our reconnaissance pilots. Then we took off into five-tenths cloud at 3,000m. We stayed just below the clouds and got close to the airfield before we were spotted. Five kilometres from the target we were met by a

131
On Sunday 22 June 1941, at 03.15hrs, Germany launched its attack against Russia; Operation 'Barbarossa' had started. Amongst the highly experienced Luftwaffe units participating, were I and II Gruppe of ZG26 — III Gruppe operated at that time in the Mediterranean area. Photographed on an airfield 'somewhere in Russia' in early June 1941, are several Ju52/3ms, a Fieseler Fi156 Storch and Bf110E-1 3U+CB, belonging to the Gruppenstab of I/ZG26. Note that the engines of the Bf110 have been removed from the wings.

wall of fire. We could see the airfield we had to attack but all around us the Flak exploded. One can be an old and experienced pilot but that sort of sight always gives you the shivers until the order to attack comes. When it did we checked our weapons and the instruments and then dived. Diving from 3,000m we picked up a lot of speed before we reached the witch's cauldron. Shells exploded to the right and to the left, and in the middle of our formation, but we didn't hear them any longer. Feverishly all we thought about was the attack. Each of us concentrated on our targets. The airfield came nearer and nearer, the details became clearer. In the middle of the attack you had to be careful not to collide with one of your comrades.

'Closer and closer we got, the ground rushing up towards us . . . 500m . . . 300m . . . 100m — and now our weapons bark. The Zerstörergruppe roared over the airfield in a wide arc only a few metres high. Here and there we could see enemy aircraft catching fire. Then we pulled up, the formations broke up and everyone was his own boss. From every direction aircraft attacked their victims. The enemy Flak put up a heavy barrage, but they simply couldn't follow us and wherever possible one of us fired at the enemy guns . . . but we paid most of our attention to destroying the aircraft on the ground.

'There's one, half in and half out of the hangar. We dive towards it. Suddenly the wireless operator shouts through the intercom: "Take care. Pull up." Automatically one follows the order and sees the fin of another aircraft passing very near just below. We've had our share of luck!

'The operator shouts again: "Achtung! Enemy fighters from left!" So, now the enemy fighters are here as well. But it doesn't matter. Down below everything is on fire, one can see explosions and clouds of fire rising higher and higher. As if in a dream we see one of our own machines trailing smoke. He's been hit by the enemy Flak and heads for home. But the aircraft loses height, gets lower and lower and there, it's crashed. At this moment the man under the heaviest pressure is the Kommandeur who must stay cool and must reassemble his Geschwader and send it on its course towards the base — which at last he manages. On the return journey we look closely at our machines. Most of us have received hits but the engines, oil pressure and temperatures are all right. The results of

the attack make us proud: 48 aircraft destroyed on the ground, three in the air and only one of our own aircraft lost — what a shame this one couldn't have been filmed . . . .

'Sometimes we were somewhat envious of our fighter pilots. Time and time again they scored victories and flew over the airfield, waggling their wings. Every victory was seen as a personal success for them — this was not the case with the Zerstörer. None of us became famous — we didn't expect to. What matters in war is not individual glory but the overall result.

'Early in September 1941 Soviet aircraft crossed East Prussia at night and got as far as Berlin. At first nobody could find out from which airfield they had originated, so our Geschwader got the order to find out

and to take matters in hand. Ten of our Zerstörer took off. In the area where the enemy bombers might have taken off there were several airfields. Each one was overflown by our reconnaissance aircraft and each of them was carefully observed but no Soviet bombers were to be seen. Only one airfield looked suspect, so we flew back to look it over again. From a height of 1,500m nothing was to be seen but large numbers of flak emplacements. Had the bombers been well camouflaged or had they left the airfield? We had to get down to the deck to find out, so as soon as we were out of sight of the airfield we dived to low level and turned back towards it flying fast and as low as possible. Flashing over trees and houses, we got back unobserved and roared over.

132
The Luftwaffe is having a field-day. Taken completely by surprise, the Russians are fighting back desperately, but to no avail. Hundreds of Russian aircraft are destroyed on the ground, many airfield installations heavily damaged. This Bf110E-1 belonging to the 1st Staffel of an unknown unit, is throwing-up a lot of dust before commencing its take-off run.

133
This Bf110C received extensive damage in the starboard wing during a mission on the Eastern Front. The fabric is hanging down in shreds, exposing the badly mangled inner part of the wing. A rather unhappy looking mechanic is surveying the damage, probably thinking about the hard work that is in store for him and his colleagues.

134
During every major campaign, the Luftwaffe reconnaissance units played an important role. During Operation 'Barbarossa', one of these units was Aufklärungsgruppe 33. This Bf110E-1, coded 8H+WK, photographed during its landing run, belongs to 2/(F)33. This Staffel flew long-range reconnaissance missions in Russia, in 1941, for Panzer Gruppe 3. In 1942, the unit was redesignated 2/(H)33 reverting to the rôle of short-range reconnaissance. When, on 2 February 1943, the battle for Stalingrad ended — with disastrous results for the German 6th Army — some aircraft of 2/(H)33 remained near the city. Their crews, along with all the other surviving German soldiers, went into Russian captivity.
Bundesarchiv

134

135
Two Obergefreite and a
Hauptmann (middle) are looking
at the map, before going on a
mission over Russia. Behind
them is a Bf110E-2 coded
KE+YF. Next to the aircraft is the
starter trolley. *Bundesarchiv*

136
Two groundcrew members in the
process of installing the 57mm
armoured windscreen. At right
part of the pilot's back armour
can be seen. *Bundesarchiv*

'We kept our eyes open as we went and, sure enough, there between the farm buildings we could see undercarriages and gleaming propellers. The aircraft had been perfectly camouflaged with branches and heather and from above we could have searched forever! Now we had seen enough. In all we had counted some six or seven aircraft but surely there were more. We quickly flew back to report on what we had seen.

'Ten Zerstörer took off the next morning, heavily laden with bombs, with the order to destroy this wasps' nest. "Achtung. Get ready to drop the bombs." We had anticipated this order from the leading aircraft. Automatically the bombsight was switched on, the weapons armed, the instruments checked. Everything all right! Then the order came through the earphones: "Barbara one, Barbara two, Barbara three . . ." and the Zerstörer dived down, rushing towards the airfield. Then the order, "bombs away!". Ten aircraft dropped their bombs simultaneously on the airfield. Bombs rained down. "Pull up slowly, left turn," was the next order. We could hear the bombs exploding below us and in the ensuing panic dived for a low-level attack. We attack each of the enemy aircraft . . . shells explode all around us but we do not care . . . smoke clouds rise from the earth, parts of aircraft fly through the air, houses and hangars fall down . . . 16 enemy aircraft are set on fire . . . . At last the Kommandeur sets us on a course towards our base and once again we take stock: two men wounded, two aircraft with engine trouble having to fly home on one engine . . .'.

In the same propagandistic and 'heroic' vein Hauptmann Johannes Kiel went on to describe other Zerstörer actions, like the following episode:
'One day I had to fly cover over our foremost armoured units with three aircraft. We had been given the order "freie Jagd" — which meant that I had to prevent enemy bombers attacking our tanks. I had been flying over the Panzers at a height of 2,000m but couldn't see any enemy aircraft and began to get bored. I flew some distance away over the front and started hunting cars . . . I found a lorry on which six men were sitting. They saw me and immediately jumped off and took cover. I fired at the truck and immediately an immense smoke cloud rose upwards and I heard a terrific explosion. I was only just able to pull my aircraft up, the truck had been loaded with ammunition! When the smoke cloud dispersed, all that could be seen was a huge crater. Just then my wireless operator tapped me on my shoulder: "Enemy bombers, setting course for our lines!".

'That set the alarm bells ringing — what about our tanks? Immediately I flew back towards them and, sure enough, saw the enemy aircraft — nine abreast. There we were on the deck while they were much higher — 2,000m — and getting close to the front. We climbed as quickly as possible, hoping we'd make it before they did. 500m, 1,000m, 1,500m — another 500 and we'd be OK.

'Just in time we reached the enemy bombers and as we began the attack we saw 10 Soviet fighters 500m higher giving top cover to the bomber formation. Ten fighters against three Zerstörer! It was a hopeless situation, but we couldn't let the enemy bombers drop their bombs.

'Luckily it seemed that the fighters hadn't noticed us yet because they stayed where they were. The three of us went at the bombers — one to the right side of the formation, one in the middle and I went for the bomber on the left, which I attacked from 50m. Immediately a thick smoke cloud trailed out, the bomber pulled up and then spiralled downwards.

'Amazingly enough the enemy fighters still hadn't noticed us. But the bombers were too close to the tanks for me to pick my target. I just flew through the formation and sprayed bullets all over forcing the bombers to scatter. My two companions had both shot down a bomber each, but the enemy fighters had spotted us and started down. We dived and roared away, our mission complete. Three enemy bombers had been shot down and we had scattered the enemy bomber formation . . .'.

But after the initial German successes the fearful Russian winter set in: 'During these *Abwehrschlachten* (ground attack operators) our men and aircraft had to give their utmost. Even during snowstorms and at temperatures of −40deg our engineers had to change engines standing in the open. No mean task! We hardly flew any attacks against enemy airfields in the rear any more. Like everybody else the Zerstörern were used for immediate defence against the enemy onslaught . . .'

Low-Level over Russia

Zerstörergeschwader 1 was activated for the second time early in 1942. The first two groups were simply the first two groups of the former Schnellkampfgeschwader 210 and operated Bf110 fighter-bombers against the Soviet forces.

Kriegsberichter George Haller of Luftwaffe-Kriegsberichter-Kompanie (mot) 6 flew in a 110 during a low-level attack and wrote this report which was published in the German propaganda magazine *Der Adler* for 19 May 1942:

'The operations briefing is over. The Kommandeur rises. At the neck of his leather jacket glistens the silver edge of his Knight's Cross. His orders and instructions were short and to the point. Few words are needed anyway because the men surrounding him are veterans of many combat missions, usually more than a hundred in the east alone, more during the Norwegian and French campaigns. The crews are used to each other, they know what is expected from them and they know what counts.

'On their fur jackets some of them wear the insignia which gave the Gruppe its name and which is also painted in bright colours on the aircraft fuselages: the wasp with the giant staring eyes and the wide mouth which seems so avid to devour anything in its path. This humorous warpaint had become well known when the unit was titled SKG 210.

'Today's mission is directed against Soviet reinforcements and troop concentrations in front of the German positions. They've been trying to break through for several weeks attacking again and again at various points without getting any worthwhile results. . . . The cold weather brings about many difficulties and makes it necessary to run up the engines for a long time. Also the weather reports are unfavourable: fog at 50m above the ground hampers the possibility to orientate oneself, but we will fly, as we must fly!

'The Gruppe has got used to many things and today we fly under circumstances

137
Bf110F-1 of II/SKG210 on an airfield in Russia in 1942. Beneath the fuselage is a twin ETC500 and beneath the wings the twin ETC50 bomb racks. The unit was renamed II/ZG1 during 1942. In April 1943, II/ZG1 transferred to Sicily, to aid the other Zerstörergruppen in their struggle against an overwhelming enemy, during the final stages of the African campaign.

which formerly would have been thought practically impossible. . . . The Schwarm speeds at 400km/hr over wide plains, over burned out villages, over small oak woods, along deep gorges which cut through the plateau. Sometimes it flies in a row, sometimes in line abreast, sometimes at the edge of the low-hanging snow-clouds, sometimes only a few metres above the ground. The guns and cannon are loaded and ready and below the wings hang the fragmentation bombs feared by the Soviets. . . .

'The invisible band of the wireless unites everybody, the Kommandeur, the pilots, the wireless operators. But silence still reigns in the air, nobody is speaking. Burning farm-houses appear in sight, guns stand in the terrain below, Flak covers the roads, tanks roll across the fields; we are over the front. The Schwarm climbs to an attacking height, from which everything looks as small as toys indifferently scattered over the terrain by a clumsy giant in a playful mood. And yet this is the front and every mission is cruelly serious.

'A railway runs across our flight-path — we're now right at the front line and the German troops fire recognition signals. On the other side of the line lie the Soviets, the target of our attack. As we dive down the tanks, guns and soldiers which a moment ago still looked like toys suddenly come alive. Our armament hammers away, fragmentation bombs hail down. Running away doesn't help the soldiers, nor does flattening themselves against the ground because every movement and every man is clearly visible against the white snow cover. Again and again the German aircraft attack from all sides, one following the other diving down, pulling up and diving down again. Machine gun flashes, anti-aircraft shell explosions, the light of firing guns and 2cm tracers greedily claw at us, but the *Wespenschwarm* (swarm of wasps) does not let up until the attacking Soviet troops have been destroyed and the German positions held.

'And still the unit goes on. Through the earphones comes: "Cäser to Paula, columns to the left, check to find out if enemy". Cäser is the call sign of the Kommandeur and the order is directed to his wingman who immediately veers away. The order was superfluous as the column had already been sighted and even before Paula's answer comes through had been recognised as enemy. Again everything

happens at lightning speed. . . . The Bf110s hug the ground to get as close as possible without being seen. Then the storm breaks loose over the totally surprised column. In panic horses try to break away, carts turn over and drag along drivers and crews. Spitting fire the Zerstörer roar down on the Soviet transport vehicles. At the head of the column there is a large truck, a fat target. We fly towards it. Nerves are taut — fractions of seconds become hours in which one's own fate and that of the enemy is decided. The hand is on the stick, the eyes at the gunsight and the thumb on the button which fires the guns. Now the thumb pushes the button those five millimetres.

138
Port vertical fin of a Bf110 — flown by a successful pilot — displaying 16 aerial victories. The nationalities of the hapless enemy pilots are: Polish, French, Yugoslavian, unknown and Russian.

139

After the invasion of Russia in June 1941, Schnellkampfgeschwader SKG210 was very active. They became famous for their dive- bombing attacks on airfields, Flak positions, bridges, railways, etc. This Bf110C-4 of SKG210 has its engines tested shortly before taking off.

140

In 1942, SKG210 was renamed ZG1. The II Gruppe of ZG1 stayed in Russia and saw action there until March 1943. The Bf110F-1 shown has the customary ETC500 bomb rack installed beneath the fuselage. Note the difference in design of the Wasp insignia, compared with the foregoing photographs.

141

A Bf110F-1 of II/ZG1 on an Italian airfield, after the unit's return from Russia in April 1943. The pilot is revving-up the engines prepartory to take-off. II/ZG1 was the last Gruppe of the Geschwader using BF110s. At the end of 1944, the unit traded them for Bf109s and was renamed III/JG76. Note again the difference in design of the Wasp insignia.

Four explosions vibrate through the airframe and already we are over the truck. A quick glance below: did the volley strike home? As we zoom up we see a giant flame shooting out of the truck, and a black column of smoke billows out. It must have been a fuel truck. The smoke column rises up to the cloudbase, amidst the desolate landscape, a good orientation point in this monotonous countryside where it is difficult to navigate.

'The "Wasps" only turn back when there's nothing left of the Soviet column but wrecked and burning vehicles. . . . Our ammunition is nearly spent; we must go home. Suddenly two black specks appear on the horizon out of the fog. "Fighters in direction six!" Dammit, this we could do without. No more ammunition and now fighters. On top of that our left engine is no longer running smoothly. It seems to have been hit. We dive down very low. Are the fighters coming nearer? Have they spotted us? Are they friend or foe? Our left engine starts to overheat, blue smoke escapes from the cowling, and it runs slower and slower. We have to gain height so that we can limp back to base — but this will make us even more vulnerable to attack. Where are those fighters? There! Approaching us very fast.

'We're in luck! They're friendly aircraft from our group and they fly cover for us on our way home. Landing is a bit difficult on one engine and there are a few hairy moments before we touch down but it's OK: we're home!'

141

A Staffel in Figures

Just to show the amount of action a typical Zerstörerstaffel saw in the early war years, here are details of all missions flown by 5/ZG26 from its first war mission on 10 May 1940 up to 23 August 1941 when the Staffel was posted back to Germany for a rest period at Celle.

After these details all the awards and decorations given to Staffel personnel are noted.

The following abbreviations are used:

AS (*Alarmstart*)=Alarm Scramble
BA (*Bewaffnete Aufklärung*)=Armed
   reconnaissance
BF (*Begleitschutz für
Fallschirmspringer*)=Escorting paratroops
BW (*Bombenwurf*)=Bombing mission
FJ (*Freie Jagd*)=No specific target
IS (*Infanterieschutz*)=Infantry protection
JS (*Jagdschutz*)=Interception mission
KB (*Kampfverband begleitet*)Bomber Escort
TA (*Tiefangriff*)=Low level mission

No	Date	Start Time	Home airfield	Target	Mission/Victories

Missions against the enemy in Belgium and France

No	Date	Start Time	Home airfield	Target	Mission/Victories
1	10.5.40	5.25	Kaarst	Charleroi	KB
2	10.5.40	17.05	Kaarst	Charleroi	KB
3	11.5.40	14.03	Kaarst	Charleroi	KB
4	12.5.40	11.55	Kaarst	Charleroi	KB
5	12.5.40	18.45	Kaarst	Charleroi	KB
6	13.5.40	11.37	Kaarst	Antwerpen	KB
7	14.5.40	10.35	Kaarst	Charleroi	KB
8	14.5.40	19.10	Kaarst	Charleroi	KB
9	15.5.40	6.25	Kaarst	Namur	KB
10	15.5.40	13.27	Kaarst	Namur	KB, 3
11	16.5.40	15.35	Kaarst	Mons	KB
12	17.5.40	5.50	Kaarst	Charleroi	KB
13	17.5.40	17.34	Kaarst	Charleroi	KB
14	18.5.40	16.50	Kaarst	Chambrai	KB, 2
15	19.5.40	15.33	As	Chambrai	KB
16	26.5.40	15.30	St Trondt	Abbeville	KB
17	27.5.40	13.10	St Trondt	Calais	KB
18	28.5.40	11.30	St Trondt	Ypern	KB
19	29.5.40	17.30	St Trondt	Roubaix	KB
20	31.5.40	17.00	Lille	Dunkirk	FJ, 5
21	1.6.40	6.10	Lille	Dunkirk	KB
22	1.6.40	15.35	Lille	Dunkirk	KB, 1
23	2.6.40	10.39	Lille	Dunkirk	KB
24	5.6.40	6.11	Lille	Paris	KB
25	5.6.40	14.27	Lille	Paris	KB

No	Date	Start Time	Home airfield	Target	Mission/Victories
26	6.6.40	16.40	Lille	West Paris	KB
27	7.6.40	6.30	Lille	West Paris	KB
28	7.6.40	16.00	Lille	West Paris	KB
29	8.6.40	10.10	Lille	West Paris	KB
30	8.6.40	15.40	Lille	West Paris	KB
31	9.6.40	6.35	Lille	West Paris	KB
32	9.6.40	15.00	Lille	West Paris	KB
33	9.6.40	19.36	Lille	Rouen	KB
34	10.6.40	10.33	Lille	Le Harve	KB
35	10.6.40	18.05	Lillers	Le Harve	KB
36	11.6.40	12.35	Lillers	Le Harve	KB
37	14.6.40	11.09	Lillers	Le Harve	KB
38	14.6.40	19.45	Lillers	Le Harve	FJ, 1
39	17.6.40	17.50	Rouen	Rennes	KB
40	18.6.40	13.45	Rouen	Le Bourget	KB
41	19.6.40	11.53	Rouen	Le Bourget	KB
42	20.6.40	19.14	Rouen	Cherbourg	KB
43	21.6.40	13.45	Rouen	Rennes	KB
44	22.6.40	12.56	Rouen	Le Bourget	KB

142
Hauptmann Ralph von Rettberg, photographed in the cockpit of his Bf110 at the time when he was Gruppenkommandeur of II/ZG26. Von Rettberg saw action in France, the Battle of Britain, the invasion of Crete and later on in Russia. He was awarded the Knight's Cross on 2 August 1941 for acts of bravery during the battle for Crete. After flying 100 missions his score was four aircraft shot down and 12 destroyed on the ground. At the end of the war his total score would be eight aircraft shot down. On 1 May 1945, with the rank of Oberstleutnant, he was placed at the disposal of the 7th US Army and released from captivity on 12 July 1945.
Ralph von Rettberg

No	Date	Start Time	Home airfield	Target	Mission/Victories

Missions against England

No	Date	Start Time	Home airfield	Target	Mission/Victories
45	12.8.40	8.25	Crecy	SW England	KB
46	15.8.40	15.02	St Omer	South London	KB
47	15.8.40	18.52	St Omer	North London	KB
48	16.8.40	16.57	St Omer	North London	KB
49	18.8.40	13.30	St Omer	North London	KB
50	18.8.40	17.34	St Omer	North London	KB, 2
51	24.8.40	15.44	St Omer	North London	KB, 4
52	26.8.40	15.12	St Omer	North London	KB
53	29.8.40	16.07	St Omer	North London	KB, 1
54	30.8.40	11.22	St Omer	Oxford	KB
55	30.8.40	16.20	St Omer	Oxford	KB
56	31.8.40	8.21	St Omer	London	KB, 1
57	31.8.40	17.58	St Omer	North London	KB
58	2.9.40	8.11	St Omer	North London	KB, 1
59	2.9.40	16.32	St Omer	North London	KB
60	3.9.40	10.28	St Omer	North London	KB, 1
					KB, 1

143
A Bf110D-0 of II/ZG26 ready for take-off from an airfield in Italy. In the background, at right, is an Italian Savoia-Marchetti SM81 *Pipistrello* (Bat). *Bundesarchiv*

144
A Kette of Bf110C-4s flying over Budapest. The aircraft belong to a Zerstörerschule as can be judged from aircraft DE+MP, carrying the numeral 1 on the lower part of the nose section. *Bundesarchiv*

No	Date	Start Time	Home airfield	Target	Mission/Victories
61	6.9.40	9.02	St Omer	Kingston	KB
62	7.9.40	17.04	St Omer	Kingston	KB
63	9.9.40	17.21	St Omer	London	KB
64	11.9.40	15.41	St Omer	London	KB
65	15.9.40	14.30	St Omer	London	KB
66	15.9.40	18.02	St Omer	London	KB
67	25.9.40	11.49	St Aubin	Plymouth	KB
68	25.9.40	16.50	St Aubin	Bristol	KB
69	26.9.40	11.16	St Aubin	Bristol	KB
70	26.9.40	18.16	St Aubin	Southampton	KB
71	27.9.40	13.48	St Aubin	Bristol	KB
72	27.9.40	17.55	St Aubin	Bristol	KB
73	28.9.40	15.15	St Aubin	Portsmouth	KB
74	30.9.40	11.40	St Aubin	Yeovil	KB
75	30.9.40	16.45	St Aubin	Yeovil	FJ, 2
76	1.10.40	11.05	St Aubin	Yeovil	KB
77	5.10.40	14.03	St Aubin	Portsmouth	KB
78	7.10.40	15.57	St Aubin	Yeovil	KB, 1
79	10.10.40	12.44	St Aubin	Portsmouth	KB
80	27.10.40	17.09	St Aubin	Portsmouth	BW
81	28.10.40	16.45	St Aubin	Portsmouth	BW
82	29.10.40	17.10	St Aubin	Portsmouth	BW
83	1.11.40	12.30	St Aubin	Portsmouth	BW
84	5.11.40	13.15	St Aubin	Portland	BW
85	6.11.40	15.00	St Aubin	Southampton	BW
86	7.11.40	14.45	St Aubin	Southampton	BW
87	7.11.40	17.05	St Aubin	Southampton	BW

Missions against Yugoslavia, Greece and Crete

No	Date	Start Time	Home airfield	Target	Mission/Victories
88	6.4.41	5.40	Sofia	West exit from Serre	BW
89	6.4.41	10.24	Sofia	Skopje	KB
90	6.4.41	15.12	Sofia	Krusevac, munitions factory	BW & KB
91	8.4.41	6.05	Sofia	Nis railway	TA
92	12.4.41	15.00	Skoplje	Retreating troops	BW
93	14.4.41	13.00	Skoplje	Retreating troops	BW
94	20.4.41	15.50	Larissa	Piraeus Harbour	KB & TA, 5

145
Dramatic view of Bf110G-2s of II/ZG76 diving down on a railway emplacement. The nearest aircraft carries the code 2N+BP and has the 300-litre fuel tanks and *Wurfgeräte* 21 installed beneath the wings. Beneath the fuselage is a ventral gun tray, containing two MG151/20 cannons. *Bundesarchiv*

No	Date	Start Time	Home airfield	Target	Mission/Victories
95	21.4.41	15.35	Larissa	Athens — Piraeus	KB
96	22.4.41	5.48	Larissa	Tatoi/Athens airport	TA
97	22.4.41	15.37	Larissa	Salamis	KB
98	23.4.41	5.35	Larissa	Tatoi airport	TA
99	23.4.41	11.03	Larissa	Retreating troops	TA
100	23.4.41	17.33	Larissa	Retreating troops	BW
101	24.4.41	9.48	Larissa	Salamis	KB
102	24.4.41	16.20	Larissa	Piraus	TA
103	25.4.41	17.30	Larissa	Corinth airport	TA
104	26.4.41	5.20	Larissa	Flak Corinth	TA & BW
105	25.4.41	10.02	Larissa	Corinth	BF
106	27.4.41	15.45	Larissa	Corinth	BW
107	14.5.41	7.00	Argos	Athika	TA
108	17.5.41	5.20	Argos	Canea airport	AS
109	17.5.41	6.25	Argos	Enemy bombers	BA
110	18.5.41	16.20	Argos	Crete Canea/Crete airport	TA
111	19.5.41	12.00	Argos	Canea/Crete airport	BW
112	20.5.41	7.00	Argos	Crete	BF & TA
113	20.5.41	14.43	Argos	Crete	AP & TA
114	21.5.41	4.31	Argos	Flak Crete	BF & TA
115	21.5.41	15.40	Argos	Flak Crete	TA & escorting Ju52
116	22.5.41	7.15	Argos	Artillery positions Crete	TA
117	22.5.41	13.00	Argos	Anti-ships Crete	BF
118	22.5.41	16.58	Argos	Flak Crete	BF
119	23.5.41	15.25	Argos	Rethimnon/Crete	BF
120	24.5.41	7.05	Argos	Crete	FJ
121	24.5.41	7.55	Argos	Crete	FJ
122	24.5.41	13.25	Argos	Crete	FJ
123	25.5.41	5.05	Argos	Crete	TA & escorting Ju52
124	25.5.41	11.45	Argos	Crete	TA & escorting Ju52
125	25.5.41	14.18	Argos	Crete	BW
126	26.5.41	7.30	Argos	Crete	Escorting Ju52
127	27.5.41	7.23	Argos	Crete	Escorting Ju52
128	28.5.41	14.55	Argos	Heraklion/Crete	Escorting Ju52
129	28.5.41	9.20	Argos	Rethimnon/Crete	Escorting Ju52

146
Rear gunner of a Bf110G-2 behind his twin 7.92mm MG81Z Zwilling machine guns. This weapon was built by the Mauser armaments company and a total of 46,000 MG81Z machine guns were manufactured from 1940 until 1944 at the Obendorf factory alone. The weight of the weapon was 12.9kg, it could fire 1,600 rounds/min and the muzzle velocity was between 705 and 875m/sec, depending on the ammunition used.

147
Rear view of the MG81Z Zwilling machine guns, installed in a Bf110G-2. At left and right are the ammunition belts and on top of both machine guns the chutes for the empty belts. Note armour plates in the extreme rear of the cockpit. *Bundesarchiv*

No	Date	Start Time	Home airfield	Target	Mission/Victories
130	28.5.41	14.55	Argos	Heraklion/Crete	BW
131	29.5.41	6.07	Argos	Rethimnon Airport	BW
132	29.5.41	17.15	Argos	Sphakia/south coast of Crete	BW
133	30.5.41	12.10	Argos	Isle of Gaudos	BW
134	31.5.41	6.30	Argos	Rethimnon/Crete	Escorting Ju52
135	31.5.41	13.00	Argos	Rethimnon/Crete	Escorting Ju52
136	1.6.41	8.40	Argos	Sphakia, Loutro	TA

Missions against Russia

No	Date	Start Time	Home airfield	Target	Mission/Victories
137	22.6.41	2.55	Suwalki	Alytus	BW
138	22.6.41	8.35	Suwalki	3 airfields near Luna	TA, 1
139	22.6.41	13.05	Suwalki	6 airfields near Lida	TA & BW
140	22.6.41	17.05	Suwalki	6 airfields near Lida	TA & BW,
141	23.6.41	3.15	Suwalki	Wilna	KB
142	23.6.41	7.30	Suwalki	Lorry column, Wilna	TA & BW
143	23.6.41	14.05	Suwalki	Lorry column, Wilna	TA & BW
144	23.6.41	17.28	Suwalki	Railways	TA & BW
145	24.6.41	12.15	Suwalki	Molodetschno	TA
146	24.6.41	17.32	Suwalki	Minsk station	JS
147	25.6.41	3.30	Suwalki	Lorry column, Minsk	JS
148	25.6.41	9.41	Suwalki	Lorry column, Minsk	TA
149	26.6.41	4.15	Suwalki	Around Minsk	BA
150	26.6.41	13.28	Suwalki	Around Minsk	BA
151	26.6.41	13.35	Suwalki	Around Minsk	BA
152	26.6.41	15.39	Suwalki	Lorry column	TA
153	27.6.41	12.03	Suwalki	Lorry column	TA
154	27.6.41	12.45	Suwalki	Lorry column	TA
155	29.6.41	10.56	Suwalki	Around Minsk	BA
156	1.7.41	10.45	Wilna	Dünaburg, Ostrowno	TA
157	1.7.41	16.05	Wilna	Dünaburg, Ostrowno	TA
158	2.7.41	18.45	Wilna	Borissow	BA, 2
159	3.7.41	9.30	Wilna	Borissow	BW
160	4.7.41	3.45	Wilna	Dünaburg	BW
161	4.7.41	11.52	Wilna	Polozk	BW
162	5.7.41	11.30	Wilna	Around Polozk	FJ
163	5.7.41	18.15	Wilna	Around Polozk	FJ
164	6.7.41	10.15	Wilna	Around Polozk	FJ, 5
165	6.7.41	18.48	Wilna	Around Polozk	FJ
166	7.7.41	15.47	Wilna	Around Ulla	FJ
167	8.7.41	7.50	Sloboda	Newel	TA
168	8.7.41	12.30	Sloboda	Newel	KB
169	8.7.41	19.10	Sloboda	Newel	TG
170	9.7.41	8.10	Sloboda	Around Polozk-Czina	JS
171	9.7.41	19.00	Sloboda	Wbelis	KB
172	10.7.41	13.30	Sloboda	Welikije-Luki	BW
173	10.7.41	18.45	Sloboda	Witebsk	KB
174	11.7.41	2.50	Sloboda	Around Czisna-Ulla	FJ
175	11.7.41	18.30	Sloboda	Around Ulla-Rudrija	KB & FJ
176	12.7.41	14.33	Sloboda	Smolensk	KB
177	12.7.41	19.25	Sloboda	Czisna Airport	FJ
178	13.7.41	2.57	Sloboda	Around Witebsk	FJ
179	13.7.41	4.50	Sloboda	Around Witebsk	FJ
180	13.7.41	7.00	Sloboda	Around Witebsk	FJ, 1
181	13.7.41	??.??	Sloboda	Around Smolensk	FJ
182	13.7.41	11.46	Sloboda	Around Smolensk	FJ

No	Date	Start Time	Home airfield	Target	Mission/Victories
183	13.7.41	15.35	Sloboda	Around Czisna	FJ
184	13.7.41	17.35	Sloboda	Around Czisna	FJ
185	14.7.41	2.48	Sloboda	Around Smolensk	BA & TA
186	14.7.41	8.30	Sloboda	Around Smolensk	BA & TA
187	14.7.41	18.00	Sloboda	Lorry column	BA & TA
188	15.7.41	3.30	Sloboda	Around Smolensk	BA & TA
189	15.7.41	4.55	Sloboda	Around Smolensk	BA & TA
190	16.7.41	19.15	Pskov	Around Leningrad	BA & TA
191	17.7.41	16.45	Pskov	Staraja-Russa	BW
192	18.7.41	11.55	Pskov	Staraja-Russa	BW, 2
193	19.7.41	8.05	Pskov	Around Leningrad	KB
194	19.7.41	12.30	Pskov	Around Leningrad	KB & AS
195	19.7.41	19.45	Pskov	Around Leningrad	KB
196	20.7.41	3.10	Pskov	Around Leningrad	BW
197	20.7.41	8.00	Pskov	Railways	TG
198	21.7.41	3.35	Pskov	Lorry column	TG
199	21.7.41	11.53	Pskov	Around Leningrad	FJ, 1
200	22.7.41	17.05	Pskov	Around Leningrad	FJ
201	23.7.41	7.35	Pskov	Around Dorpat	BA & TA
202	23.7.41	12.15	Pskov	Staraja-Russa	BW
203	23.7.41	18.15	Pskov	Ljuban bei Leningrad	BW
204	24.7.41	17.10	Pskov	Reval airfield	BW
205	25.7.41	3.10	Pskov	Reval airfield	BW
206	25.7.41	8.45	Pskov	Nogorad	BA, 1
207	25.7.41	14.55	Pskov	Bologol	KB
208	26.7.41	9.20	Pskov	Jadrowo	BW
209	26.7.41	16.00	Pskov	Jadrowo	BW
210	27.7.41	3.50	Pskov	Around Kury	BW
211	27.7.41	8.15	Pskov	Kury airfield	BW
212	27.7.41	15.40	Pskov	Columns	BW
213	27.7.41	19.15	Pskov	Near Sawina-Cholm	BW

148
The crew of a Bf110G-2/R3 of ZG1 are jubilantly welcomed by members of the groundcrew and flying personnel, after achieving the Gruppe's 500th victory. The aircraft is powered by two Daimler Benz DB605B-1 engines and the armament consists of two nose-mounted Rheinmetall-Borsig 30mm MK108 cannon, two Mauser 20mm MG151/20 cannon mounted beneath the cockpit floor and two Mauser MG151/20s in a ventral gun tray beneath the fuselage. Note the dirty appearance of the wing upper surface and the flare chute opening beneath the gunner's compartment. *Bundesarchiv*

No	Date	Start Time	Home airfield	Target	Mission/Victories
214	30.7.41	9.45	Sarudinje	Jadrowo airfield	BW
215	30.7.41	17.00	Sarudinje	Jadrowo airfield	BW, 1
216	31.7.41	12.00	Sarudinje	Jadrowo airfield	TG
217	1.8.41	9.28	Sarudinje	Around Nowcorow	TG & JS
218	1.8.41	15.45	Sarudinje	Around Ilmensee	KB
219	2.8.41	6.05	Sarudinje	Around north Peipussee	BA & BW
220	2.8.41	17.15	Sarudinje	Reval airfield	BW
221	4.8.41	6.00	Sarudinje	Reval airfield	BA
222	5.8.41	15.45	Sarudinje	Reval airfield	BA
223	6.8.41	8.30	Sarudinje	Stremelanje	BW, 1
224	7.8.41	11.35	Sarudinje	Siwerskaja	BW, 1
225	10.8.41	4.05	Sarudinje	Luga	BW
226	10.8.41	10.05	Sarudinje	Luga	BW
227	10.8.41	13.45	Sarudinje	Volossovo	BW
228	11.8.41	17.08	Sarudinje	Flakstellungen	BW
229	11.8.41	19.00	Sarudinje	Kikerino station	BW
230	12.8.41	10.20	Sarudinje	Sipovo airfield	BW, 1
231	12.8.41	16.30	Sarudinje	Sipovo airfield	BW
232	13.8.41	7.30	Sarudinje	Koplja	SF & IS
233	13.8.41	12.00	Sarudinje	Lorry column	BW
234	13.8.41	17.30	Sarudinje	Koplja	BA
235	14.8.41	6.00	Sarudinje	Siwerskaja	BW
236	14.8.41	9.30	Sarudinje	Kingissepp	FJ
237	15.8.41	10.33	Sarudinje	Kingissepp	FJ, 1
238	15.8.41	13.50	Sarudinje	Kingissepp	FJ
239	15.8.41	17.55	Sarudinje	Two airfields, near Kingissepp	TA
240	16.8.41	9.55	Sarudinje	Krasnowardeysk airfield	BW
241	16.8.41	12.20	Sarudinje	Krasnowardeysk airfield	TA
242	16.8.41	18.00	Sarudinje	Krasnowardeysk airfield	TA
243	17.8.41	9.15	Sarudinje	Krasnowardeysk airfield	TW
244	17.7.41	12.55	Sarudinje	Krasnowardeysk	BW
245	18.8.41	17.10	Sarudinje	Around Leningrad	FJ
246	19.8.41	10.30	Sarudinje	Around Leningrad	FJ
247	20.8.41	16.15	Sarudinje	Flak Krasnowardeysk	BW

149
BF110G-2 of an unknown unit. The aircraft still carries the tropical filter, mounted on the starboard engine. *Bundesarchiv*

For actions during these 247 missions, a total of 149 decorations and awards was given:

Oberfeldwebel Kurt Rochel	19.5.40	Iron Cross 2nd Class
Oberfeldwebel Fritz Herber	19.5.40	Iron Cross 2nd Class
Hauptmann Eberhard d'Elsa	5.6.40	Iron Cross 2nd Class
Oberleutnant Artur Niebuhr	5.6.40	Iron Cross 2nd Class
Oberleutnant Kurt Specka	5.6.40	Iron Cross 2nd Class
Oberfeldwebel Hans Müller	5.6.40	Iron Cross 2nd Class
Oberfeldwebel Josef Auer	5.6.40	Iron Cross 2nd Class
Unteroffizier Theodor Pietschmann	5.6.40	Iron Cross 2nd Class
Unteroffizier Gerhard Gröhl	5.6.40	Iron Cross 2nd Class
Unteroffizier Mathias Nicoley	5.6.40	Iron Cross 2nd Class
Unteroffizier Reinhard Immig	5.6.40	Iron Cross 2nd Class
Unteroffizier Klaus Theisen	5.6.40	Iron Cross 2nd Class
Unteroffizier Werner Raabe	5.6.40	Iron Cross 2nd Class
Unteroffizier Hermann Rößler	5.6.40	Iron Cross 2nd Class
Feldwebel Hermann Schönthier	17.6.40	Iron Cross 2nd Class
Unteroffizier Heinz Lohoff	20.6.40	Iron Cross 2nd Class
Unteroffizier Willy Schöffler	20.6.40	Iron Cross 2nd Class
Unteroffizier Willi Hübner	20.6.40	Iron Cross 2nd Class
Obergefreiter Rudolf Franke	20.6.40	Iron Cross 2nd Class
Oberleutnant Theodor Rossiwall	30.6.40	Iron Cross 1st Class
Oberfeldwebel Kurt Rochel	8.7.40	Iron Cross 1st Class
Oberleutnant Reinhard Hubel	14.7.40	Iron Cross 2nd Class
Gefreiter Karl Andrea	14.7.40	Iron Cross 2nd Class
Oberleutnant Heinz Ihrcke	18.7.40	Iron Cross 1st Class
Oberfeldwebel Fritz Herber	18.7.40	Iron Cross 1st Class
Oberleutnant Artur Niebuhr	11.8.40	Iron Cross 1st Class
Hauptfeldwebel Karl Danielsen	11.8.40	Iron Cross 2nd Class
Oberfeldwebel Gustav Cramer	11.8.40	Iron Cross 2nd Class
Unteroffizier Georg Leinfelder	23.8.40	Iron Cross 2nd Class
Obergefreiter Günter Franke	23.8.40	Iron Cross 2nd Class
Oberleutnant Kurt Specka	24.8.40	Iron Cross 1st Class
Hauptmann Eberhard d'Elsa	4.9.40	Iron Cross 1st Class
Unteroffizier Theodor Pietschmann	5.9.40	Iron Cross 1st Class
Unteroffizier Willy Schöffler	5.9.40	Iron Cross 1st Class
Unteroffizier Klaus Theisen	5.9.40	Iron Cross 1st Class
Oberleutnant Reinhard Hubel	11.9.40	Iron Cross 1st Class
Feldwebel Hermann Schönthier	11.9.40	Iron Cross 1st Class
Feldwebel Hans Müller	11.9.40	Iron Cross 1st Class
Feldwebel Josef Auer	11.9.40	Iron Cross 1st Class
Unteroffizier Hermann Rößler	11.9.40	Iron Cross 1st Class
Unteroffizier Georg Leinfelder	11.9.40	Iron Cross 1st Class
Unteroffizier Heinz Lohoff	11.9.40	Iron Cross 1st Class
Oberleutnant Theodor Rossiwall	26.9.40	Ehrenpokal für besondere Leistung im Luftkrieg
Gefreiter Heinz Müller	28.9.40	War Service Cross 2nd Class with Swords
Leutnant Fritz Mittler	30.9.40	Iron Cross 1st Class
Unteroffizier Heinz Schrodt	30.9.40	Iron Cross 1st Class
Unteroffizer Reinhard Immig	30.9.40	Iron Cross 1st Class
Unteroffizier Gerhard Gröhl	30.9.40	Iron Cross 1st Class
Unteroffizier Mathias Nicoley	30.9.40	Iron Cross 1st Class
Unteroffizier Franz Beckel	30.9.40	Iron Cross 1st Class
Obergefreiter Günter Franke	30.9.40	Iron Cross 1st Class
Obergefreiter Walter Munz	30.9.40	Iron Cross 2nd Class
Feldwebel Heinz Zeidelhack	11.10.40	War Service Cross 2nd Class with Swords
Leutnant Lothar Heckert	21.10.40	Iron Cross 2nd Class
Unteroffizier Ernst Berger	21.10.40	Iron Cross 2nd Class
Unteroffizier Walter Munz	28.10.40	Iron Cross 1st Class
Oberfeldwebel Franz Walbert	1.11.40	War Service Cross 2nd Class with Swords
Feldwebel Willi Leichsenring	1.11.40	War Service Cross 2nd Class with Swords
Unteroffizier Fritz Kalkhoff	1.11.40	War Service Cross 2nd Class with Swords
Hauptmann Theodor Rossiwall	25.3.41	Operational Flying Clasp in Silver
Oberleutnant Kurt Specka	25.3.41	Operational Flying Clasp in Silver
Oberfeldwebel Hans Müller	25.3.41	Operational Flying Clasp in Silver
Oberfeldwebel Theodor Pietschmann	25.3.41	Operational Flying Clasp in Silver
Oberfeldwebel Hermann Rößler	25.3.41	Operational Flying Clasp in Silver
Leutnant Heinrich Spitzner	25.3.41	Operational Flying Clasp in Bronze
Oberfeldwebel Fritz Herber	25.3.41	Operational Flying Clasp in Bronze
Oberfeldwebel Hermann Schöntheir	25.3.41	Operational Flying Clasp in Bronze
Feldwebel Georg Leinfelder	25.3.41	Operational Flying Clasp in Bronze
Feldwebel Heinz Lohoff	25.3.41	Operational Flying Clasp in Bronze
Feldwebel Horst Reiß	25.3.41	Operational Flying Clasp in Bronze
Unteroffizier Franz Beckel	25.3.41	Operational Flying Clasp in Bronze
Unteroffizier Günter Franke	25.3.41	Operational Flying Clasp in Bronze
Hauptmann Eberhard d'Elsa	12.4.41	Operational Flying Clasp in Bronze
Oberfeldwebel Kurt Rochel	12.4.41	Operational Flying Clasp in Bronze
Feldwebel Gerhard Gröhl	12.4.41	Operational Flying Clasp in Bronze
Unteroffizier Ernst Berger	12.4.41	Operational Flying Clasp in Bronze
Unteroffizier Alois Kommans	12.4.41	Operational Flying Clasp in Bronze
Unteroffizier Rudolf Franke	12.4.41	Operational Flying Clasp in Bronze
Unteroffizier Willi Hübner	12.4.41	Operational Flying Clasp in Bronze
Unteroffizier Willy Schöffler	12.4.41	Operational Flying Clasp in Bronze
Oberfeldwebel Heinz Paas	20.4.41	War Service Cross 2nd Class with Swords
Oberfeldwebel Theodor Pietschmann	23.4.41	Operational Flying Clasp in Gold
Leutnant Dietrich Oldenburg	5.5.41	Iron Cross 2nd Class
Unteroffizier Fritz Müller II	5.5.41	Iron Cross 2nd Class
Unteroffizier Erich Robel	5.5.41	Iron Cross 2nd Class
Gefreiter Rudolf Blandowski	5.5.41	Iron Cross 2nd Class
Oberfeldwebel Hermann Schönthier	11.5.41	Operational Flying Clasp in Silver
Feldwebel Heinz Lohoff	25.5.41	Operational Flying Clasp in Silver
Leutnant Dietrich Oldenburg	25.5.41	Operational Flying Clasp in Bronze
Unteroffizier Karl Grininger	25.5.41	Operational Flying Clasp in Bronze
Unteroffizier Erich Robel	25.5.41	Operational Flying Clasp in Bronze
Unteroffizier Walter Hamacher	25.5.41	Operational Flying Clasp in Bronze
Gefreiter Werner Scheskat	25.5.41	Operational Flying Clasp in Bronze
Gefreiter Peter Jung	25.5.41	Operational Flying Clasp in Bronze
Unteroffizier Fritz Müller	27.5.41	Operational Flying Clasp in Bronze
Gefreiter Rudolf Blandowski	27.5.41	Operational Flying Clasp in Bronze
Grefreiter Willi Zahn	28.5.41	Operational Flying Clasp in Bronze
Grefreiter Gerhard Kohr	28.5.41	Operational Flying Clasp in Bronze
Leutnant Fritz Mittler	29.5.41	Operational Flying Clasp in Silver
Unteroffizier Karl Grininger	1.6.41	Iron Cross 2nd Class
Unteroffizier Walter Hamacher	1.6.41	Iron Cross 2nd Class
Unteroffizier Otto Stein	1.6.41	Iron Cross 2nd Class
Gefreiter Werner Scheskat	1.6.41	Iron Cross 2nd Class
Gefreiter Gerhard Kohr	1.6.41	Iron Cross 2nd Class
Gefreiter Peter Jung	1.6.41	Iron Cross 2nd Class
Gefreiter Willi Zahn	1.6.41	Iron Cross 2nd Class
Gefreiter Dietrich Herrmann	1.6.41	Iron Cross 2nd Class
Hauptmann Theodor Rossiwall	23.6.41	Operational Flying Clasp in Gold
Feldwebel Eduard Brandl	25.6.41	War Service Cross 2nd Class with Swords
Feldwebel Hans Weber	25.6.41	War Service Cross 2nd Class with Swords
Feldwebel Kurt Gärtner	25.6.41	War Service Cross 2nd Class with Swords
Unteroffizier Fritz Kipf	25.6.41	War Service Cross 2nd Class with Swords
Unteroffizier Günter Wellnitz	25.6.41	War Service Cross 2nd Class with Swords
Flieger Heinz Willberg	27.6.41	Operational Flying Clasp in Silver
Oberfeldwebel Hans Müller I	12.7.41	Operational Flying Clasp in Gold
Gefreiter Hans Jani	14.7.41	Operational Flying Clasp in Bronze
Leutnant Peter Bosselmann	16.7.41	Iron Cross 2nd Class
Gefreiter Alois Slaby	16.7.41	Iron Cross 2nd Class
Oberleutnant Franz Smolle	20.7.41	Operational Flying Clasp in Bronze
Unteroffizier Heinz Lorenz	20.7.41	Operational Flying Clasp in Bronze
Oberleutnant Heinz Ihrcke	24.7.41	Operational Flying Clasp in Gold
Flieger Heinz Wilberg	24.7.41	Operational Flying Clasp in Gold
Gefreiter Gerhard Kohr	24.7.41	Operational Flying Clasp in Silver
Gefreiter Willi Zahn	26.7.41	Operational Flying Clasp in Silver
Gefreiter Dietrich Herrmann	26.7.41	Operational Flying Clasp in Bronze
Gefreiter Martin Prätorius	26.7.41	Operational Flying Clasp in Bronze
Oberleutnant Franz Smolle	28.7.41	Iron Cross 2nd Class
Leutnant Heinrich Karras	28.7.41	Iron Cross 2nd Class
Unteroffizier Franz Fischbach	28.7.41	Iron Cross 2nd Class
Unteroffizier Heinz Lorenz	28.7.41	Iron Cross 2nd Class
Gefreiter Karl Stephan	28.7.41	Iron Cross 2nd Class
Gefreiter Martin Prätorius	28.7.41	Iron Cross 2nd Class
Gefreiter Hans Jani	28.7.41	Iron Cross 2nd Class
Unteroffizier Walter Hamacher	30.7.41	Operational Flying Clasp in Silver
Unteroffizier Rudolf Blandowski	30.7.41	Operational Flying Clasp in Silver
Hauptmann Theodor Rossiwall	2.8.41	Knight's Cross
Feldwebel Heinrich Strobl	2.8.41	War Service Cross 2nd Class with Swords
Unteroffizier Johann Sebus	2.8.41	War Service Cross 2nd Class with Swords
Oberfeldwebel Hermann Schönthier	16.8.41	Operational Flying Clasp in Gold
Oberfeldwebel Hans Müller	20.8.41	Ehrenpokal für besondere Leistung im Luftkriege
Oberfeldwebel Hermann Schönthier	1.10.41	Ehrenpokal für besondere Leistung im Luftkriege
Oberfeldwebel Theodor Pietschmann	1.10.41	Ehrenpokal für besondere Leistung im Luftkriege
Oberfeldwebel Hermann Rößler	1.11.41	Ehrenpokal für besondere Leistung im Luftkriege
Oberfeldwebel Hermann Rößler	20.8.41	Operational Flying Clasp in Gold
Unteroffizier Werner Scheskat	21.8.41	Iron Cross 1st Class
Leutnant Peter Bosselmann	21.8.41	Operational Flying Clasp in Bronze
Feldwebel Otto Stein	21.8.41	Operational Flying Clasp in Bronze
Unteroffizier Franz Fischbach	21.8.41	Operational Flying Clasp in Bronze
Gefreiter Alois Slaby	21.8.41	Operational Flying Clasp in Bronze

150
After returning from a mission, the pilot of this Bf110G-2 of 13(Z)/JG5 is welcomed by 'Lockheed' one of the staffel pet dogs; the other pet dogs were 'Herdla' and 'Bamse'. This was the reason why the unit was nicknamed the *Dackelstaffel* ('Dackel' is a diminutive form of 'Dachshund').

151
A crane is used to mount the airscrew on the newly installed Daimler Benz DB605A-1 engine in the port wing of this Bf110G-2. The groundcrew was a hard working and skilled group of men, keeping the aircraft in flying condition. They earned no fame or medals and they often had to work in severe weather conditions.

150

151

152
The airfield of Herdla (Norway), served as home base for 13(Z)/JG5 after the unit left Kirkenes, near the Finnish border, in February 1944. On 30 March 1944, while protecting a German sea-going convoy under attack by British Beaufighters, Bf110G-2 1B+EX disappeared near Utsima, while chasing a British aircraft. No trace was ever found of the aircraft or its crew, pilot Oberfeldwebel Albert Mack and Unteroffizier Rolf Möbius, the wireless-operator/gunner.

152

100

153
A Kette of Bf110G-2s of 13(Z)/JG5 banking to port, while flying over a Norwegian fjord, near Stavanger. The aircraft in the middle, coded 1B+AX, is probably flown by the Staffelkapitän, Hauptmann Herbert Treppe.

154
Due to the extremely low temperatures on the *Eismeer* (Polar Sea) front, the aircraft were parked in makeshift hangars, to protect them from the cold and sudden snowfall. Here a Bf110G-2 of 13(Z)/JG5, 1B+FX, is seen leaving its hangar.

155
Before taking off, Bf110G-2 1B+FX taxied to the refuelling area. The 300-litre fuel tanks are filled-up for a long flight over the icy waters of these northern regions. Note fuel bowser on the left and small letter F on the inboard ETC50 bomb rack, beneath the port wing. The dirty and worn appearance of the aircraft is very much in evidence.

156
Bf110G-2s of 13(Z)/JG5, operated on the Eismeer front until late 1944 — by that time the unit was renamed 10/ZG26. One of their many tasks was the attacking of the Allied sea-going convoys en route to Murmansk. The Bf110G-2, 1B+LX, is flown by Oberleutnant Ziegenhagen. Note the combination of ETC50 wing-mounted bomb racks, and 300-litre fuel tanks. In the rear of the cockpit is a MG81Z Zwilling machine gun.

157
Another task of 13(Z)/JG5 was the protection of German naval vessels, operating in Northern waters. Here Bf110G-2 is on patrol over a small group of German warships.

157

158
A large formation of Bf110G-2s of 13(Z)/JG5 on a flight over the snow covered and mountainous region of Northern Norway, in June 1944.

158

159
To provide German troops fighting in the northern regions with urgently needed supplies, convoys sailed daily to the ice-free ports of the Polar Sea. Constantly harassed by Russian aircraft, these convoys needed fighter protection. Zerstörer were also used for the same purpose and JG5 could provide both. A Kette of two Bf110G-2s and a Bf110F-3 (nearest aircraft) is on its way to meet an inbound German convoy.

160
Fighter and Zerstörer units were stationed all along the Norwegian coast, protecting the German sea-going convoys bringing in vital supplies for the German troops stationed in those regions. Here a Bf110G-2 is pushed back into its hangar after returning from a mission.

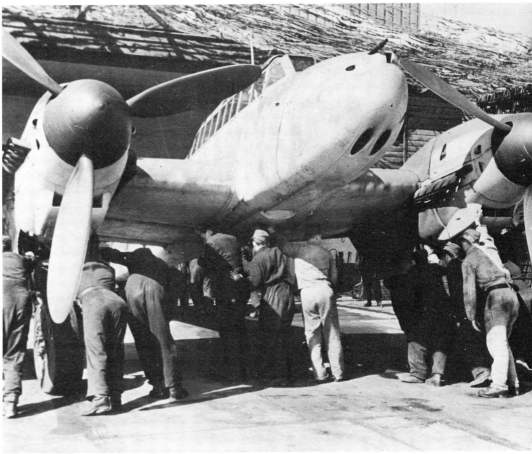

161

162

161

A Bf110C-4 on patrol over an inhospitable and mountainous part of Norway. Aircrew having to force-land in such an area could only hope that somebody who saw them going down would notify the rescue teams.

162

Bf110E-1, LN+KR, WNr 4113, of 1(Z)/JG77 force-landed at Pajala, Sweden, on 1 September 1941 and returned to Germany on 20 September 1941. On 15 December 1941 the aircraft crashed near the airfield of Rovaniemi, Finland, killing the pilot, Leutnant Eberhard

Reichel, and the wireless-operator/gunner, Gefreiter Günther Boehmer.

163

Oberleutnant Felix Brandis, Staffelkapitän of 10(Z)/JG5, at left and his wireless-operator/gunner Feldwebel Braus, feeding a 'third' crew member 'Putzi'. Behind both men is a Bf110E-2. On 2 February 1942, while flying in appalling weather conditions, both Brandis and Braus, crashed with their aircraft on to the frozen Lake Pjaw. Brandis was killed instantly and Braus, seriously wounded, was transported to a nearby hospital.

163

164

Smiling crew of a Bf110G-2 after returning from a successful mission. Both men are wearing different types of life-jacket and these are proof that their mission was near or over the icy waters on the Norwegian coast. Note strange marking left of the Balkenkreuz: a black number 1.

165

Main landing gear wheel change for a Bf110G-2. The massive size of those wheels can easily be judged, when compared with the groundcrew members. Note spinner marking, removed external dust filter and landing light in the wing leading edge. At the right of the underwing 300-litre fuel tank, part of the ETC50 bomb rack is visible.

166

166

In November 1940 Stab/ZG76 and III/ZG76 were stationed at Stavanger, Norway, their mission: the defence of the airspace over Northern Norway. Since both units saw little action it was decided to use them as fighter-bombers, acting against enemy shipping near the English coast. To expand the range of their aircraft, 300-litre fuel tanks were installed beneath the wings; the same tanks as the ones installed on Junkers Ju87s. The flying time of the Bf110s was augmented to 3hr 30min. It was even possible to mount 900-litre fuel tanks beneath the wings and expand the flying time of the Bf110 to 5hr 30min; Oberstleutnant Grabmann once flew a Bf110 from Stavanger to Kirkenes, a flying distance of 2,000km! The matter was taken-up with the Messerschmitt works who decided to instal attachment points beneath the wings of Bf110 night-fighters as standard equipment. *Walter Grabmann*

A Kommandeur on Night-Fighting

During the war, Hauptmann Werner Streib wrote a story about night-fighting for the *Jahrbuch der Luftwaffe 1942*, the Luftwaffe's yearly almanac for 1942. After consulting with Herr Streib, nearly 40 years later he found that, with some minor alterations, the story was still valid. Here it is:

' "Any questions about the weather?" I ask the crews and thus terminate the nightly briefing by our meteorologist. "How cold is it at 6,000m?" asks one of our youngest. Everybody laughs — he only wants to know if he can leave one of his pullovers at home. But that will not be possible as our scientist mentions the figure of −30degC. We also listen to our own *Wetterflieger* (weather reconnaissance pilot) so that we know the actual meteorolgical conditions, visibility at ground level and at different heights, the haze levels, height of cloudbase and cloud tops, amount of cloudiness, the wind speed and direction at various levels, the times of moonrise and setting, the weather over England and above all the way we can expect the weather to change during the night. We are especially interested to know if the weather could suddenly deteriorate — if visibility could get worse or if there is a possibility of fog, because it's not very nice to return from a mission with fuel for only 15min on board and then to have to execute a difficult landing in bad weather. After all we do not fly airliners but very fast fighters, with the corresponding differences in handling and amount of fuel carried. You don't get much chance to land at an alternative airfield and you have to act fast and accurately.

'Finally, I make some points about the mission — drawing on our recent experiences — and then I leave the room with a *Weidmanns Heil* (hunters greeting). The crews, officers, non-coms and soldiers go to the *Bereitschaftsräume* (ready rooms) and the *Oberwerkmeister* (ground crew chiefs) who had also been present at the weather-briefing, give the latest orders near the aircraft. The Oberwerkmeister are the connecting link between the flying crews and the ground crews. They have lived through the successes and failures of their units from the start of the war — and they have watched many a pilot and wireless-operator team take-off for the last time.

'These old foxes like to be present at the weather-briefings: on one hand they want to know what can be expected from the

167
Hauptmann Werner Streib was among those who pioneered night-fighting in 1940. On 20 July 1940 he shot down an RAF Whitley bomber and was officially credited with the first night victory of World War 2. He became Gruppenkommandeur of I/NJG1 in October 1940, the month in which he was credited with his 10th victory. His total score would amount to one daylight and 65 night victories. He replaced Major Wolfgang Falck as Geschwader-kommodore of NJG1 on 1 July 1943. In March 1944 he was appointed Inspector of the night fighter force. After the war, in 1956, he joined the new German Luftwaffe and retired in 1966 with the rank of Generalleutnant. *Werner Streib*

weather and the enemy; on the other hand, we, the flying personnel, like to have them there. I cannot overpraise the groundcrew whose responsibilities — especially for a night-fighter unit with its alarm take-offs — are enormous. Poor control and servicing of the aircraft can mean the death of the crew — at night no emergency landings are possible. Either one reaches the airfield in an aircraft more less in working order or one has to bale out, a not too appealing prospect on a dark night. Everything is important, from engine to wireless installation. If the latter becomes unserviceable through poor servicing or enemy fire then only luck will let the crew find an airfield before the fuel runs out. Then there is the dubious pleasure of being shot at by one's own AA, as time after time one gets into their area without wanting to. . . .

'In the meantime it has got dark outside: it's 21.30hrs. "Will 'the other side' honour us with a visit tonight?" I ask Oberleutnant Th while we don our flying overalls and hang our torches around our necks. "It's about time they did", he answers and thus expresses the wishes of the nightfighters, which are totally opposite to those of the civilian population! But somehow tonight I have the feeling that something is in the air. It is misty out and seven-tenths cloud — slowly disappearing — starts at 1,000m. I go over to the squadron HQ and suddenly an order comes by telephone: *"Erste Welle Sitzbereitschaft"* (first wave on standby).

Everybody runs towards his aircraft. I myself climb into my good old "D". My trustworthy *erster Wart* (chief mechanic), a Feldwebel, has reported it to be ready. My wireless operator also gets aboard and once more checks his wireless set. He's an experienced gunner/operator in both day and night fighting. We haven't got any victories together yet because he has only recently replaced my usual companion, Oberleutant Sch who was wounded when I got my tenth victory.

'My mechanic helps me get into the parachute harness and seat belts. I move the stick about and check the elevator and rudders; with the help of a torch I check the trim setting, propeller pitch setting, position of flaps and of the hinged intake fairing, the temperature gauges and other important gauges. Everything is in good order or "ready to dive" as we say. All over the place the reports "Sitzbereitschaft carried out" are given. . . .

'We have now been in Sitzbereitschaft for a considerable time and I am beginning to doubt that anything will happen. Perhaps the English turned back at the coast or went for another target? How many times have we sat in Sitzbereitschaft only to be stood down after an hour . . . to be ordered back again half an hour later . . . and so on the whole night long. . . . We'd prefer a mission to that nightlong Sitzbereitschaft. One cannot get any sleep anyway — even if we could lie down — when one is expecting an

168
Major Wolfgang Falck was also one of the pioneers of night-fighting and stayed in command as Geschwaderkommodore of NJG1 until 1 July 1943. On that day Major Werner Streib, here still a Hauptmann, took over command and Wolfgang Falck returned to Berlin.
Wolfgang Falck

alert. But once we get off the ground, one victory makes one forget all those nights spent in fruitless waiting. The worst months are behind us now — November, December, January and February. The difficult weather conditions during winter and the continuous icing-up of the aircraft made flying very trying. Readiness would start at 17.30hrs and go on till 09.00hrs the next morning. Icy winds swept over the airfield and the aircraft became freezing to the touch. The ground-crews had a terribly hard time.

'But now I cannot let my thoughts wander any longer because the music which had been coming from the loud-speakers suddenly stops and we hear the order "First wave to take-off". The martial music played immediately after the order is lost in the noise of starting engines. My mechanic shouts encouragement, shuts the canopy, jumps down and gives the "clear" signal with his torch. The airfield lights — absolutely necessary for take-offs — have been switched on. We use these sparingly so as not to give away our airfield location to the Tommies.

'I am the second to take-off. In front of me an aircraft lifts off and turns off its position lights. I too open up the engines and run into the dust cloud whirled up by my predecessor. I move faster and faster over the tarmac, lift off and turn on to my course while at the same time switching off my position lights, retracting the under-carriage and setting flaps and propeller, arming the machine guns and so on. I am accompanied to the right and to the left by the bluish-reddish exhaust-flames of my two engines which are working well. I can tell this by ear, and confirm it by a glance at the instruments. The airfield, once again engulfed in darkness, lies far behind. I have put on the oxygen mask, radio communications are good, I am climbing fast, flying through separate tattered clouds, now there's no time to lose. (Later, after landing again, I asked for the starting times. Within three minutes, six machines had taken off, a good performance even for daylight fighters. But then this take-off didn't need as much concentration as some during pitch-black nights; the moon was an excellent source of illumination.)

'I had been in my hunting area only a short time when things started to happen. I could see searchlight activity to the north — what a shame it wasn't in my area. I thought about it and flew closer — *Donnerwetter!* The fingers of light had caught an Englishman. The aircraft glistened in the sea of light like a gem. It's probably the first chance that Leutnant R has had to show that he can fly and shoot. His first encounter with the enemy for which he has waited such a long time — so go to it!

'I opened up my engines to get closer, especially as nothing was going on in my area. At last Leutnant R attacked and the Englishman answered with every weapon at his disposal. One could clearly see the arcs of fire against the night sky. Now the usual duel between fighter and rear-gunner began as in the meantime I closed to within 300m of the enemy. I could recognise the type from this distance — it is a Handley Page Halifax and it is defending itself well — Leutnant R's first attack had proved fruitless. Still that wasn't the end of the world — I too had scored my first victory at night after my second attack. I throttled down the engines and turned towards the

169
Hauptmann Werner Streib, Gruppenkommandeur of I/NJG1, is helping Major Wolfgang Falck, Geschwaderkommodore of NJG1, into his flying suit. Note the connecting points for the upper arm elements of the heating system, situated in the lower left arm of the flying suit. This photo was taken on 30 June 1943 at the airfield of Deelen, Holland. *Wolfgang Falck*

enemy without firing and stayed in the dark on a parallel course to the Englishman about 200m away. One never knows! I had done this before and when Leutnant B with two engines out of action could no longer attack and baled out I was able to fall on the Tommy and rob him of his victory by shooting him down.

'I became restless. Why wasn't Leutnant R attacking for a second time? Has he been wounded? Just as I am about to attack I see him moving into position behind the Englishman. A first exchange of fire . . . and the Halifax flies apart. "Congratulations R" I shout, "your first victory". My operator who had seen it all, has congratulated him too — but mutters as well that the victory could have been ours. Nevertheless I was perfectly happy with the result as without doubt the Tommy was in the other hunting area. I also know what it means for a crew to obtain a victory at last after many fruitless missions. Leutnant R had been especially

keen. He often flew under difficult weather situations but until now he had not had hunter's luck. Wherever he flew, there seemed to be no Englishmen in the vicinity, while it was said of me that I had a magnet which attracted the Tommies!

'The whole affair had lasted only a few seconds and when it was over I flew back to my area watching the Englishman burn on impact and the bombs explode one after another. Unknown to me Leutnant R's aircraft had been so badly damaged during the second attack that the pilot, after having fainted for a short time, had to bale out. His radio operator had been killed — a heavy price for victory. Should I have attacked anyway? That's a question too late to be answered.

'It is shortly before 23.00hrs; suddenly there is searchlight activity in my own area. Carefully I approach. Well done, searchlights — with their arms of light they have caught an aircraft and held on to it. I push

170
In late 1940, Major Wolfgang Falck invited five crew members of a downed British bomber to lunch as guests at the HQ of Stab/NJG1 in Arnhem, Holland. The German Oberleutnant, standing next to the British airman with the bandaged eye, was the pilot who shot down the unfortunate crew. Fourth from the right is Wolfgang Falck. *Wolfgang Falck*

171
In 1943, Oberstleutnant Wolfgang Falck organised the *Befehlsstelle Ost des Inspekteurs der Nachtjäger* (Command Post East of the Directorate of Night-Fighters). From this command post, the aerial defence of Rumania and its oilfields at Ploesti was conducted. The photograph shows Falck about to leave Rumania and return to Germany. Behind both men is Falck's Bf110E-1/U1 night-fighter, coded G9+AA. *Wolfgang Falck*

172
After receiving last-minute instructions from a despatch-rider, the pilot of this Bf110G-2 will start-up the engines, commence his take-off run and will be off on another nocturnal mission.

173
Every night the Allies were sending hundreds of bombers over Germany. The Germans had to counter these nightly bombing raids with night fighters Various types of aircraft were used in the night fighter role, the majority being C-, D-, E- and F-versions of the Bf110, culminating in the night fighter *par excellence*: the Bf110G-4. This Bf110C returns from a nocturnal mission, at daybreak.

the nose down, having already opened up the throttle and set the propeller pitch. The engines are turning at full rpm, the airspeed indicator shoots upwards, the aircraft gives everything it has got.

'I approach very swiftly, watching the familiar glittering in the glare of the searchlights, but it is only as I get closer that I realise that the enemy is flying exactly the opposite course. To shoot now doesn't make sense and we flash by each other only a few metres apart. I have already throttled down, and turn after him opening up the engines again. I get behind him, he becomes larger and larger in my visor, a giant bird, another Halifax. The red lights on my instrument board show that my weapons are ready to shoot. So I push the buttons and my weapons hammer away. Close behind the Enlishman's tailplane I pull out. . . . "Where is he?" I shout into my microphone, then I see him again — his right engine is on fire, and his roundel glows spookily in the light of the flames. He goes down in a left hand spiral. I fly alongside him, being very careful — many times we have seen a rear-gunner in a burning machine firing away very accurately — they are very courageous. I do not want to make a second attack and say to my operator: "Perhaps we can capture him intact; I think he is going to try an emergency landing".

'But things turn out differently. The Tommy doesn't get any lower than 2,000m and instead of landing he jettisons his bombs and heads back towards England, his engine fire getting less and his speed increasing. This is not what we bargained for so I attack again and this time the bomber loses a burning wing and crashes. I don't see anyone bale out.

'Three minutes later I see searchlight activity to the south. There's a burning torch in the sky — not a flare, an aircraft. Immediately afterwards I see the explosion on the ground. Good old Oberfeldwebel H, I did not expect otherwise from him — it's his fourth night victory. Even as I watch the searchlights light up in my area again — things are really happening tonight! I take up the correct tactical position, watch the fingers of light probing the night sky: suddenly one of them stops, others join it — they must have caught something! As I get nearer I see another British aircraft. Unsuccessfully he tries to escape from the searchlights by diving, climbing and turning. What was it that a shot-down Englishman once said? "We were caught in the searchlights and the AA didn't fire so I shouted to the crew, 'Nightfighters! I hope you've written your wills!' and before I'd finished speaking I could feel the bullets hitting the aircraft!'

'I'm in a good attacking position but a bit high. I hurry towards the target and suddenly I'm in the searchlight beams myself. The enemy rear-gunner shoots at me and I see his tracers flying past my left wing. I crouch behind my stick, the enemy right in my gunsight but still too far away. Now! My guns fire, I zoom upwards behind the bomber's tailplane and my operator shouts: "He's burning". I just make out two men baling out. Like grapes they fall, washed in the red and white light of the searchlights and of the burning machine. Then the aircraft crashes into the ground.

'But I don't have time to watch. I have to worry about flying: the stars which just before were above me are suddenly to my left. I've been dazzled by the searchlights and I've lost my sense of direction. Quickly I react as if I was blindflying and right myself and the stars once again are where they should be!

'During the attack the Englishman must have banked and because I was concentrating on the target and automatically following his movements I hadn't noticed the movement. Everything happens so much faster in action: we have obtained victories in less than a minute.

'I light up my instruments; temperatures are normal, oil and fuel pressures also. "No hits this time", I think. Later on the ground two hits were found, but they were slight. Half an hour later Leutnant F shoots down his first enemy, pressing the attack so strongly that he hits the enemy aircraft and damages his own badly. Unsure of making a safe landing he made his operator bale out — he landed safely in an oak tree and appeared half an hour later at the *Gefechtsstand* (squadron HQ). . . .

'In one hour we had shot down five bombers. . . .

'The ground looked like a battlefield. Aircraft wrecks keep burning for hours. Now and then bombs explode. I continue flying until my fuel is exhausted but no more Englishmen show up. As I land my mechanic receives me with blinking lights. After the engines have been shut down he clambers upwards and opens the canopy for me. From the ground he has been able to observe some of the victories. He heartily congratulates my operator and me. It pleases him enormously to be able to paint two more stripes upon the fin. They are night victories numbers 11 and 12. . . .'

Werner Streib ended the war as an Oberst with a total of 66 victories to his name. Of those 65 were obtained at night.

174
Bf110G-4/R3 found by American troops near the Autobahn going into Munich. The aircraft is parked near a wooded area and the nearby Autobahn was used as a runway. These final production aircraft were equipped with the latest version of the aerial array for the FuG220B Lichtenstein SN2, nose-mounted Mk 108 cannons and redesigned fresh-air opening for the cockpit heating system. Above the MG151/20 cannon ports the individual letter A is visible. One of the first aircraft flying with a Lichtenstein aerial was a Bf110C-4, WNr 3296. According to the Messerschmitt-Augsburg *Monats-Meldung* nr.7, (monthly report) dated 31 July 1940, this aircraft was flown from Oberpfaffenhofen to the Messerschmitt airfield at Augsburg, for the installation of a FuG202 Lichtenstein BC antenna.

Bf110 against Mosquito

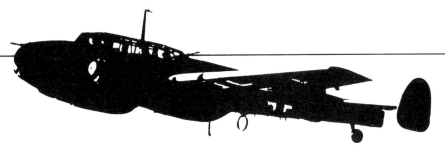

Only very few Bf110 pilots succeeded in shooting down one of the many Mosquitoes operating against Germany as bombers, night-fighters or reconnaissance aircraft. One of those was Hauptmann Paul Zorner, a Junkers Ju52/3m pilot who at his own wish was retrained as a night-fighter. Years later he recalled:

'Early in April 1944 I had taken over command of III/NJG5 in Mainz-Finthen but had not flown an operation from this airfield when, during the night of 20 April, the RAF attacked Cologne. The weather was rather poor, many layers of unbroken cloud lay over Western Germany. I took off at 01.39hrs and was ordered to fly a north-northwesterly course. From the *Luft-lagenreportagen* (situation reports) I learned that the enemy bombers had turned towards the Ruhr area and later that Cologne was the target. At that time I was near the target but could not see very much because of the bad weather. The only thing still possible was to chase one of the returning attackers who probably would fly a direct course to their bases. We'd been looking for some time and I'd just about given up hope of finding anything when my radar operator contacted a target flying much lower than ourselves. I descended but got into cloud so that I thought the chances of a successful attack were rather poor. However my operator was giving clear instructions and there was no reason not to continue the approach. I was flying on instruments and had no inkling of what the visibility was like — all around us everthing was uniformly grey.

175
Pilot and wireless-operator/gunner boarding their Bf110C-4 of NJG1. In this photograph the worn appearance of the aircraft is very much in evidence, especially near the wing root (the white number 5 is a frame number). Visible near the cockpit roof, beneath the aerial mast, is the *Antennen-Anpassungs-Gerät* (Antenna Adapter Unit) AAG1, for the *Empfänger* (Receiver) EB1, the latter being used for the reception of the radio beam, indicating the sector of approach to the airfield. Although the Luftwaffe mechanics used to wear a black overall, hence their nickname *Schwarze Männer* (Black Men), this mechanic is wearing a whitish one.
Bundesarchiv

176
The Feldwebel on the left and the two Oberfeldwebels, on the right, have been on a hunting-party with very unorthodox weapons: a pick-axe, a Very pistol and two shovels; the destination of the two hapless rabbits is very obvious! When the warning-lights, at left, light up, the Alarmrotte or -Schwarm must take-off immediately. The Bf110G-2s coded 3U+KR and 3U+HR, belong to III/ZG26. After seeing extensive action in the Mediterranean, the unit returned to Germany near the end of July 1943. The 7th Staffel of III/ZG26, to which these aircraft belong, transferred on a later date to the airfield of Wien-Seyring, was absorbed by II/ZG1 and later renamed 16/JG76. *Bundesarchiv*

177

177
Members of the groundcrew and flying personnel having a happy, but dangerous, time in the winter snow, with the aircraft's propeller turning full-speed nearby. The Bf110G-2/R3s, coded 2N+AM and 2N+LP, respectively belong to the 4th and 6th Staffel of II/ZG76. Beneath the wings are the twin rocket launchers, known as *Rüstsatz* M5, for the 21cm *Wurfgranaten*. These rocket launchers were sometimes nicknamed *Ofenröhre* (Stove-pipes). *Bundesarchiv*

178
Bf110C-4 of 9/NJG5 at Parchim (Mecklenburg) airfield, south of Schwerin, in 1943. *(Günther Wolf)*

'The target continued flying straight on, and as we got closer I moved somewhat lower than the enemy. After a few minutes my operator told me that the target must be right in front of us, so close that he could no longer give any indications about the distance. That meant that we were less than 300m away.

'At last I could make out very faintly an aircraft that looked smaller than I'd expected for the distance. I armed the guns but was very uncertain about what I had in front of me. If it was a four-engined bomber I should have seen exhaust flames but I saw nothing. At last I could make out that it was a twin-engined aircraft with a single fin — that could have been a colleague in a Junkers Ju88. But if it was he would not be flying quietly on a westerly course. I decided to stay behind him and to observe him — for us it was always a little worrying

179
On 15 May 1944, this photograph was taken at Laon-Athies airfield (France), where 9/NJG5 was stationed at that time. From left to right: Leutnant Günther Wolf and Leutnant Keller. *Günther Wolf*

180
Major Paul Zorner photographed at the time when he was the Gruppenkommandeur of III/NJG100. His experiences on 20 April 1944 are related in this chapter. *Paul Zorner*

181
Bf110G-2 with four nose-mounted 7.92mm MG17 machine guns, two 20mm MG151/20 cannons in the lower part of the fuselage and two 20mm MG151/20 cannons (*Rüstsatz* M1) in a fuselage-mounted gun tray. Above the fresh-air opening — for the cockpit-heating system — part of the aerial mast is visible.

to have a twin-engined aircraft in front. If it were a four-engined one there was no doubt that it was an enemy, but a twin-engined one led to some doubt. I got closer still. The chase had now been going on for almost 10 minutes. The fuselage seemed too short for a Ju88 and was hanging too low between the wings. At last, at a distance of some 50m, I saw that the left propeller was not moving. Everything became clear — it had to be a Mosquito trying to get home on one engine.

'The rest lasted only seconds. Slowly I pulled my machine up and let the right engine of the Mosquito traverse through my fire burst. After a few moments the Mosquito dived steeply into a cloud layer. I could not see if it crashed in flames or not. This happened at 03.00hrs — initial sighting had been at 02.50hrs. I turned back immediately and flew eastwards, reporting the probable shooting down of a Mosquito. Fifteen minutes later I landed at St Truiden in Belgium. At 06.15hrs I flew back to Mainz-Finthen where I found out that one of my Staffelkapitäne had been shot down by a Mosquito and that he had died. His two crew members had been able to parachute down and were alive.

'In the afternoon came the report that the Mosquito had crashed southeast of Antwerp at 03.06hrs. Maybe it was the same one which had sealed the fate of my comrade? . . .'.

In total Paul Zorner obtained 59 victories as a night-fighter. At the time of his encounter with the Mosquito his Bf110G-4 was still carrying the registration D5+BS from his former unit, 8/NJG3. A week later this changed to C9+AD. From the time Zorner took over this aircraft on 2 December 1943 until early July 1944 he flew 44 operational missions and obtained 42 victories. Early in July 1944 C9+AD was lost on the ground due to enemy action.

182
A row of Bf110G-2s of
5/NJG200, the nearest aircraft
being coded 8V+MN. The unit
was stationed near Odessa, on
the Black Sea, and saw action
over the Crimea and Kertsch in
1944. There they flew *Helle
Nachtjagd* and daytime Zerstörer
missions. The different
camouflage schemes are
noteworthy as are the strange
bullet-shaped objects beneath
the port wing, at left of the
300-litre fuel tanks.
Bundesarchiv

183
Very fine photograph of a
Bf110G-4/R3. The armament
consists of two 30mm MK108
cannon in the nose, two 20mm
MG151/20 cannons in the lower
part of the fuselage and two
2mm MG151/20 cannon
(*Rüstsatz* M1), in a ventral gun
tray. In the rear of the cockpit,
the so-called *B-Stand*, is a
7.92mm MG81Z Zwilling
machine gun. The 300-litre fuel
tanks are installed beneath the
wings and the radar array is a
single-pole FuG212 Lichtenstein
CI and the larger FuG220b
Lichtenstein SN2. Note the flame
dampers mounted over the
engine exhausts and the spent
cartridge deflector plate directly
behind the lower antenna strut of
the Lichtenstein SN2.

An Unusual Journey

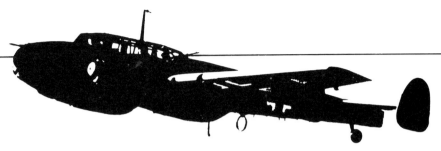

In the 29 June 1943 issue of *Der Adler* a story was published under the title 'Die ungewöhnliche Reise' ('The Unusual Journey') about a night-fighter gunner who, after being shot down, stopped a train to get back to his base. Postwar research showed that the story had been a true one. It had been written by Kriegsberichter Günther Hönicke of Luftwaffe-Kriegs-berichter Platoon 15. Here are some excerpts from the story:

'One can see the burn-wounds on his forehead. The eyebrows are also a little singed. But when one looks into the dark-brown eyes of Unteroffizier H one sees something which cannot be described. The Korporal is a wireless operator with the night-fighters and has lived through many things.

'Yes, but this time — this time it was really crazy. And that he was still alive was a real wonder, impossible to explain.

'The British bomber, a Lancaster, flew very fast. It was a dark night, the moon gave only a pale light. Only after much trouble had they succeeded in getting near to the enemy. A left turn, a right turn, dive down, then the stick fully back till the bomber became visible as a slender silhouette. The pilot, Leutnant K, was a cool calculator. He knew the good and the bad points of all English aircraft types that came over Germany. For every bomber he had a special tactic that avoided its strong points but utilised its poor points. Now they had to attack a Lancaster. He did not do things in a hurry and he waited until everything was right before he attacked. It was almost like

184
In this view of a Bf110G-2 parked on an airfield in Germany, useful details of the cockpit can be seen. In front is the 57mm armoured glass windscreen and behind the pilot the crash-bar is visible. Also parked on the airfield are Messerschmitt Bf109G-6s of an unknown fighter unit.
Bundesarchiv

the five other times he had shot down bombers. With the pressure on the button the guns began to hammer away rhythmically. The volleys flew through the dark night. The aim was good. They hit the fuselage and had to be deadly. The enemy could no longer get away.

'Unteroffizier H, the wireless operator witnessed this work of destruction, and just when he thought that the English bomber would fall, as the first flames licked from the fuselage, the inexplicable happened: he could no longer see the shadow with the white wings and the four engines. Suddenly there was a huge fireball in front of him. To the right, to the left; above, below, glaring white light. It hurts the eyes.

'He can only think "close your eyes" as with an uncanny strength the air blast pushes him from his seat towards the rear of the aircraft. And it becomes hot, hot, searing hot. The intercom does not work any longer and his flying helmet is afire burning his forehead. The aircraft dives and still there is a dazzling light.

'But then his will to live awakens. He has to get out, otherwise he's lost. Before him he sees thousands of burning and glimmering pieces. Obviously the German bullets have hit the Lancaster's bomb load which has exploded. . . .

'I must get out! With his hands he gets hold of the cabin sides and tries to pull himself out against the forces holding him back. Only 30 centimeters then he has made it! But what a long 30 centimetres! Push again . . . the cabin roof flutters away like a piece of cloth. And now he's got his torso through the opening. Quickly he steps on to the wing and dives downwards, head first . . . he somersaults — a blow against his shoulder . . . the fin! If only his arm did not hurt so much! He cannot move it and his hands are getting cold; he can hardly feel them, and he can't feel his feet at all. As he falls he somersaults again and again. Where is his parachute grip? He searches along his body with his painful arm and finally finds the grip. His flying helmet is still burning. Away with it! And now all he has to do is to pull. The white silk rustles and opens up above him. The somersaults have stopped. Slowly he oscillates downwards. How long all this takes!

'Below him he sees in the pale moonlight a shimmering surface. Water! It is April and the temperature is still low. He pulls on the lines to alter his direction of drift . . . and then his arms fall to his side to hang limply besides his body. But the water below him has disappeared. Now he can make out things. The earth, a meadow, a road, a wood. Thank God! During the last seconds things happen very fast. Yes, there are the tree-tops. The black shadows rush at him. He dives into them and rushes between two trunks. The parachute has caught in the trees. He cannot jump towards the ground, it is four metres beneath him . . . . But he cannot help himself, his hands are cold as ice, he cannot grip anything.

'But then he feels first a tickle, and then bolts of pain hit him. That's life — he can feel again. Once more he can distinguish

185
A pilot of a Bf110G-2 preparing for a nocturnal mission. Note the difference in lay-out behind the crash-bar, compared with the foregoing photograph. The red line and 45deg marking on the cockpit window are an aid to the pilot to line-up with the horizon during a diving attack.
Bundesarchiv

186
Bf110G-4/R1, equipped with the early type FuG202 Lichtenstein BC aerials. The FuG202 consisted of four antennas with four dipoles each and four reflectors. The set worked on 490 megacycles and its minimum range was 200m; the maximum range 4km (2½ miles).

187
Standard day fighter Bf110G-2, used by NJG1 in the night fighter role. Painted on the nose is the white individual letter F and beneath the fuselage is the ventral gun tray for Rüstsatz M1: two 20mm MG151/20 cannons — not installed in this view.

188
Bf110G-2/R3 with ventral gun tray and underwing mounted 300-litre fuel tanks (Rüstsatz B2), on a compass swinging platform. This platform was designed for checking the directions indicated by the compass of an aircraft, against known magnetic directions and so determining the error or deviation of the compass. This deviation is the angle between the direction in which the magnetic needle of a compass points and the magnetic North, caused by the attraction of electrical circuits and iron or steel parts of the aircraft.

between hard and soft, between thick and thin. He frees himself from his harness and slithers down and falls — and unconsciousness engulfs him.

'When he awakens again the Korporal sees a road before him. And a road must lead to houses, so he walks. The wounded shoulder still hurts. For over an hour he marches on in his socks because his boots had been flung off during his somersaults, but he doesn't reach a house. Over there is a level-crossing — there must be a telephone. Keep walking. But nothing is to be seen, only the rails which seem to lead to eternity. A full hour has gone by now and suddenly he hears behind him a deep rumbling. Two light shine over the rails: a train . . . where is his Very pistol? A Very light is pushed into the barrel. The train comes nearer. And then the red Very light shoots into the air. Shrieking and with a screeching noise the train halts. The locomotive snorts. The Korporal briefly talks to the conductor and gets on board; then the train starts off again, towards a railway station. The Korporal thinks, what an unusual journey. It started in the sky and goes on on the ground. A blissful coolness invades him when the doctor carefully puts Vaseline on his head wounds.

'But where is Leutnant K? Was he able to bale out? If only he wasn't so weak and so tired. His hands are trembling and his knees are weak. But he must call the commander, to tell him that he is still alive. If only Leutnant K is still alive.

'The phone rings at the HQ — the Korporal reports that he is back from the mission and learns that his Leutnant has been killed. He puts down the receiver and lies down on the white bed. It was an unusual journey — don't think any longer. Tomorrow everything will look different . . '

Postwar research brought to light that Leutnant K was in fact Oskar Köstler, flying from the Dutch airfield of Bergen-aan-Zee. Unteroffizier H was Heinz Huhn. Köstler and Huhn took off during the night of 9 April 1943 from Bergen airfield in their Bf110 G9+CX, WNr 4811. They belonged to IV/NJG1 normally based at Leeuwarden in Holland.

The Lancaster he shot down was Köstler's sixth and last victory. ED618 from No 101 Squadron was manned by Warrant Officer II John David Steele, pilot; Flt Sgt Michael Bennett, navigator; Sgt D'Arcy Gould, bomb aimer; Sgt John Hence, flying mechanic; Fly Off Norman Ritchie, radio-operator; Flt Sgt Stanley Grundy and Sgt William O'Brian, both gunners.

Oskar Köstler lies buried at the German War Cemetery at Ijsselsteyn, the British crew at Doornspijk, both cemeteries in Holland. Heinz Huhn survived the war and became a successful businessman. He let the author know: 'You can publish the story as it was written, that's just how it happened'.

189
Although not of the best quality, this photograph merits publication in this book, because of its rarity. With the contrails of the American bombers high above them, these Bf110G-2/R1s are climbing for altitude, in order to be able to attack the massive enemy formations. These aircraft, belonging to III/ZG26, are equipped with Rüstsatz R1, a 37mm Bordkanone BK3.7 (Flak 18) cannon, mounted beneath the fuselage. After turning the cannon 90deg around its axis, the weapon was mounted in such a way that the ejection chute for the spent cartridges faced downwards. This position also enabled the wireless-operator to load the cannon from inside the cockpit. Twelve ammunition magazines, each containing six rounds were carried in the rear cockpit.

190
Bf110E-2 night fighter, G9+BC, WNr 3475, belonging to the Gruppenstab of II/NJG1. The aircraft carries the — seldom seen on night fighters — chevron of the Gruppen-Adjutant in front of the Geschwader code. Flown by Leutnant Ullenbeck the aircraft was shot down by friendly Flak during night fighter operations, on 9 May 1941 over Schleswig Holstein. Beneath the fuselage are the loop antenna (Peilrahmen PR3) for the *Peil-Gerätsatz PeilG V*, the two dipole aerials for the *Blindlandegerät* (FuBl 2 blind-landing instrument) and between the dipole aerials the antenna for the *Bordfunkgerät* FuG25 (radio). When an aircraft flew over an area controlled by Flak units, the FuG 25 emitted a coded recognition signal enabling the gunners to identify the aircraft as friendly. Note the lengthened rear fuselage and the skywards pointing MG15 machine gun. *Alfons Schmitt*

191
Oberleutnant Helmer, flying a Bf110 night fighter, photographed by his wireless-operator. *Bundesarchiv*

192
Groundcrew chief testing the engines of a Bf110G-4 belonging to the Stab of I/NJG4. This unit adopted the well-known *Haifischmaul* (shark mouth) of II/ZG76. Note the armoured windscreen and frame numbers 4 and 5. *Bundesarchiv*

193

Last-minute testing of the starboard engine by the ground-crew chief, while other ground-crew members are standing by with fire extinguisher at the ready. On the left the crew is waiting to board their aircraft, a Bf110G-2 night fighter. Clearly visible are the exhaust flame dampers and the *Waffenwanne* 151 (ventral gun tray) beneath the fuselage. Of interest are the black painted undersides of starboard wing and engine. *Bundesarchiv*

194

Close-up view of the nose of Bf110G-4R3. Note the belly-mounted Waffenwanne which houses a pair of 20mm MG151/20 machine guns identified as Rüstsatz M1. It is interesting to note that the ammunition box for the starboard side MG151/20 contained a belt 151 with 350 rounds. The ammunition box on the port side contained a belt 151 with 400 rounds.

195

Major Wilhelm Herget, Geschwaderkommodore of I/NJG4, preparing for take-off with his Bf110G. Along with Herget are his wireless-operator and gunner. Behind him is a crash-bar guarding the pilot against serious injury in case the aircraft overturns during a crash-landing. Note crowded cockpit and wooden part of the cockpit-mounted antenna. Major Herget ended the war flying a Messerschmitt Me262 with Adolf Galland's famous unit of experts: Jagdverband JV44. He claimed 57 night and 15 daytime victories. *Bundesarchiv*

196

196

Major Werner Streib and Major Helmut Lent. Both men are wearing the *Nahnachtjäger* (short-range night fighter) flying clasp and the Knight's Cross with Oak Leaves. Werner Streib, known as the 'Father of night fighting', became Gruppenkommandeur of I/NJG1 in October 1940. On 1 July 1943 he was Geschwaderkommodore of NJG1 ending the war with the rank of Oberst and 66 confirmed victories. After the war he entered the business world but in 1956 he rejoined the German postwar air force retiring from active service in 1966 holding the rank of Generalleutnant. Helmut Lent was one of the most successful night fighter pilots with 102 night and eight day victories. After a brilliant career in which he became Staffelkapitän of 6/NJG1 on 23 September 1940 and in early 1944 Kommodore of NJG3, he died in tragic circumstances. Holder of the Knight's Cross with Oak Leaves, Swords and Diamonds, Oberstleutnant Lent was landing his Junkers Ju88C-6 on the airfield of Nordborchen, near Paderborn, on 5 October 1944. Suddenly engine trouble developed and the aircraft crashed to the ground. On 7 October Helmut Lent succumbed to his wounds and died at the age of 26. *Werner Streib*

197

Heinz-Wolfgang Schnaufer's career as a night fighter pilot had a slow start at first. He scored his first victory on 2 June 1942, but from that day on his personal score would mount steadily. As Gruppenkommandeur of IV/NJG1 he was stationed at the airfield of St Truiden, Belgium, early 1944. It was during that period that the British nicknamed Schnaufer the 'Night Ghost of St Trond' because they had a healthy respect for his daring exploits as a night fighter pilot. On 16 October 1944 he was awarded the Knight's Cross with Oak Leaves, Swords and **197** Diamonds. Appointed Geschwaderkommodore of NJG4 on 14 November 1944 he was to end the war with 121 confirmed night victories. In 1946 Schnaufer entered the family business. While driving along the Biarritz-Bordeaux road, on 13 July 1950, Schnaufer collided with a truck that came out of a side road. Seriously injured, he died in a French hospital two days later, aged 28; one of the greatest night fighter pilots of all time was no more. His mortal remains were buried at Calw in Württemberg, his home town.

199

198

198

Paul Zorner attended various aviation schools from late 1938 until early 1941. As a transport pilot, with KGzbV104, he flew various missions in Africa, Russia, Iraq, etc. On his own request he went to the night fighter school at Schleissheim, near Munich, in October 1941. In July 1942, he joined NJG2 flying Junkers Ju88s and later, the night fighter version of the Dornier Do217. He was successively appointed Staffelführer of 2/NJG3 on 6 December 1942, in March 1943 Staffelkapitän of 3/NJG3, in September 1943 Staffelkapitän of 8/NJG3, on 5 April 1944 Gruppenkommandeur of III/NJG5 and on 13 October 1944 Gruppenkommandeur of II/NJG100. He achieved his first victory on 17 January 1943 and his 59th in January 1945. He was awarded the Knight's Cross with Oak Leaves on 19 September 1944. He ended the war holding the rank of a Major and returned from Russian captivity in January 1950. Zorner is pictured here in the cockpit of a Bf110 at the Manching Night Fighter School at Ingolstadt, early in 1942. *Paul Zorner*

199

Hans-Joachim Jabs at first flew with II/ZG76 during the French Campaign and later he saw action over England. In September 1941 he was retrained as a night fighter pilot and shortly afterwards he joined NJG3. In November 1941 he became Staffelkapitän of IV/NJG1, then Gruppenkommandeur of the same unit. In March 1944 he was appointed Geschwaderkommodore of NJG1, succeeding Werner Streib in that function. He ended the war as an Oberstleutnant with 22 day and 28 night victories. After the war he started a new career as a business- and city councilman. Jabs lives a peaceful life today as a married man and father of two sons, in Lüdenscheid, Westphalia. *Hans-Jaochim Jabs*

200

During the night of 12-13 March 1941, Oberfeldwebel Hans Rasper gained his second victory in the sky over Holland. He belonged to the *Dunkelnachtjagdkommando* (night fighter command) of Bergen aan Zee and later during the war, he became a flying instructor.
Hans Rasper via Ab Jansen

201

His unfortunate victim, a Vickers Wellington Mk 1C, R1326, of No 218 Squadron came down near Opperdoes (Medemblik) in a small river. Four members of a crew of six died in the crash. At left is a German sentry guarding the wreck that has been reduced to an unrecognisable mass of twisted metal. Note that the sentry is 'loaded' with all the paraphernalia a soldier has to drag along in wartime.

202

The victorious crew alongside their Bf110E-2, G9+BM of 4/NJG1. At left Oberfeldwebel Hans Rasper, the pilot of the aircraft, and on the right his wireless-operator Unteroffizier Erich Schreiber. In November 1940 four aircraft crews of the 4th Staffel of NJG1 were stationed at Bergen, Holland. They were incorporated with the Dunkelnachtjagdkommando stationed at that time at Bergen airfield.
Hans Rasper via Ab Jansen

202

The Knight's Cross

The decoration which was most coveted by Luftwaffe pilots was the *Ritterkreuz* or, more rightly, the *Ritterkreuz des Eisernen Kreuzes*, the Knight's Cross of the Iron Cross. In fact the Iron Cross could be awarded in eight classes in the following order:

das Eiserne Kreuz 2. Klasse (second class); *das Eiserne Kreuz 1. Klasse* (first class); *das Ritterkreuz des Eisernen Kreuzes* (the Knight's Cross of the Iron Cross); *das Ritterkreuz des Eisernen Kreuzes mit Eichenlaub* (Knight's Cross with Oak Leaves); *das Ritterkreuz des Eisernen Kreuzes mit dem Eichenlaub mit Schwertern* (with Oak Leaves and Swords); *das Ritterkreuz des Eisernen Kreuzes mit dem Eichenlaub mit Schwertern und Brillianten* (with OakLeaves, Swords and Diamonds); *das Ritterkreuz des Eisernen Kreuzes mit dem Goldenen Eichenlaub mit Schwertern und Brillianten* (with Golden Oak Leaves, Swords and Diamonds); *das Grosskreuz des Eisernen Kreuzes* (the Grand Cross of the Iron Cross).

In order to bridge the considerable gulf between the Iron Cross 1st Class and Knight's Cross, Adolf Hitler instituted on 28 September 1941 the *Deutsche Kreuz* (the German Cross). The decoration had two classes: the German Cross in Gold, conferred for frequent exceptional bravery in the face of the enemy, and the German Cross in Silver which was conferred for repeated outstanding services in the leadership of troops.

Of the total of about 1,730 Luftwaffe holders of the Knight's Cross, 192 received the Knight's Cross with Oak Leaves, 41 the Knight's Cross with Oak Leaves and Swords, 12 the Knight's Cross with Oak Leaves, Swords and Diamonds, one the Golden Oak Leaves (Oberst Hans Ulrich Rudel) and one the Grand Cross of the Iron Cross (Herman Göring).

One of the many Bf110 pilots to obtain the *Ritterkreuz* was Hauptmann Rudolf Sigmund. He had joined the Luftwaffe in 1936 and became Staffelkapitän of NJG1 in the spring of 1942. It was for his actions in this function, while operating from Leeuwarden (Holland), that he was awarded the *Ritterkreuz* on 2 August 1943. The day before he had been posted to Stade near Hamburg as commander of III/NJG3 and it was at Stade that General of Night-fighters Generalmajor Josef Kammhuber himself, performed the ceremony to award Sigmund the *Ritterkreuz* on 16 August 1943. In September 1943 Kriegsberichter Walter Doelfs reported how Sigmund obtained his *Ritterkreuz*:

203
General der Nachtjäger (General of the Night Fighters) Josef Kammhuber hangs the Knight's Cross around Hauptmann Rudolf Sigmund's neck, during the medal ceremony. This event took place at Stade, near Hamburg, on 16 August 1943.
Rosemarie Boos

'Hauptmann Rudolf Sigmund is an active officer [as opposed to one drafted or in the reserve, Author]. Last year he was Gruppenadjutant with Major Lent. Today he commands a Gruppe in a night-fighter Geschwader. In the course of 112 sorties against the enemy he has shot down 26 bombers, among them 19 four-engined "heavies". He has proved to possess courage, bravery, elan and to have an extraordinary will to win. Soon after joining our Gruppe in June of last year, he shot down five heavy bombers in a very short time. Everybody called him the "Viermotorenknacker" (four-engined bomber killer). During June of this year he obtained 10 victories during only three sorties. In one night he shot down, in exactly 14 minutes, two Wellingtons and one Lancaster. Hardly half an hour later Hauptmann Sigmund shot down a fourth enemy aircraft: a Halifax. But this one gave him some trouble. The enemy had spotted the night-fighter and tried to escape to England at full speed. When the Hauptmann at last had a chance to shoot at his target, the enemy did not catch fire, despite the direct hits. The shooting must have killled or injured some of the Halifax crew because after the attack the bomber altered its course.

'Ostensibly the pilot had come to the conclusion that he could not reach the English coast. Nevertheless the Hauptmann did not stop chasing the bomber: the change of course could possibly be an attempt at deception. The bomber had to come down. A report that the weather was deteriorating could not induce the Hauptmann to let the enemy go.

'At last its fate was sealed. "Enemy aircraft down in flames", reported Hauptmann Sigmund "I'm coming home now". The Bodenstelle (ground control) crew heard this report with great relief. At the airfield the weather had become very bad. All other night-fighters had returned from their missions some time ago. They were pleased to see Sigmund here. That night he had obtained his first foursome. Four weeks later he got his 26th victory — again a Halifax, and another difficult attack.

'When Sigmund finally got the enemy bomber in his gunsights, he saw a second enemy bomber turning towards him — a potentially dangerous situation. Carefully he lost contact with the enemy bomber but did not lose sight of him. When the second bomber disappeared to the left — a favourable moment — he attacked the Halifax again. He shouted to his wireless operator: "Watch out, I'm attacking." At that moment his weapons hammered away. But at the same time his own aircraft was also hit. Was it defensive fire from the attacked bomber or had the second enemy aircraft opened fire? Sigmund did not know, all he did know is that he felt a hard blow — he must have been hit.

'He turned again towards the Halifax, which was already starting to burn, pressed the firing button and saw the aircraft disintegrate. When he saw the burning aircraft hit the ground he noticed blood running down his face. At the same time he became aware of a sharp pain in his left shoulder. He realised he'd been wounded and that he had to return to base as soon as possible. Then he noticed that flames were coming out of his left engine. "I think we will have to get out" he shouted to his operator. He did not say a word about his injuries, but when his companion wanted to jettison the cabin roof, he too was unable to raise his left arm. He had been hit as well. Two pieces of shrapnel were lodged in his left forearm. When the operator prepared to leave the aircraft he was held back by Sigmund. "Stay inside, I'll manage somehow." Several times the Hauptmann had to wipe off the blood from his forehead to prevent it running into his eyes and making it impossible for him to see his instruments — and his home airfield was still 20 minutes away. But Sigmund knew he would be able to hold out that long. The pains in his head and shoulder would not subdue him — if only the aircraft would hold out. Flames were still trailing from the stopped left engine and the aircraft had been losing height steadily. The lights of the airfield at Leeuwarden became visible. The operator fired off red Very lights continuously in order to give advance warning to the ground crews.

'Sigmund prepared for a belly landing and slid to a halt on the runway. An uncanny silence surrounded their craft as it lay with the left engine still burning. The operator was the first to get out and helped his pilot out of his seat. The Sanitäter (medical personnel) arrived almost at the same time. They wanted to put the Hauptmann on a stretcher when they saw his blood covered face but he categorically refused to let himself be carried away. He felt strong enough to walk to the Lazaret (hospital) by himself. There several pieces

204
After being awarded the Knight's Cross, Hauptmann Rudolf Sigmund had the traditional portrait taken. Little is known about his early career in the Luftwaffe, even his former wife — in a letter to the author — was unable to give any details. We know that he joined the Luftwaffe in 1936, flew Bf110s and that he was retrained as a night fighter pilot in 1941. He was posted to Leeuwarden, Holland, and became Staffelkapitän of the 11th Staffel of IV/NJG1 in 1942. After seeing extensive action over Holland, he was transferred to Stade, near Hamburg, on 1 August 1943.
Rosemarie Boos

205

Interesting view of the radio mast of a Bf110E-1 belonging to I/NJG3, the aircraft retaining the L1 code of their former unit: V/(Z)LG1. The mast has a streamlined form, is partly made of metal and wood and is insulated. The antenna wire runs from the radio mast to the starboard vertical fin and is insulated at both ends. The radio mast serves two purposes: as an auxiliary antenna for the *Zielflug-Empfänger* (radio direction finding receiver) EZ2 and as a *Bakenstab* (beacon rod) for the *Funklande-Empfänger* (radio beam receiver) EB11. The wording, *Nur hier anfassen*, means 'Only touch here'. *Bundesarchiv*

of shrapnel were removed from his forehead and shoulder.

'Hardly a fortnight has passed since that night. A few days ago Sigmund stood before us again, healthy and recovered. A white bandage covered the wound on his forehead, but his eyes again shone with the desire to attack. Notwithstanding this the doctor ordered him to take a short convalescence leave during which the news of the award of the Ritterkreuz reached him.'

Two months after being awarded the Ritterkreuz — on 31 October 1943 — Hauptmann Rudolf Sigmund attacked a formation of enemy bombers over Munich. As he returned to Stade, flying Bf110G-4, D5+AD, WNr 5560, he was shot down by friendly flak. Together with his wireless operator Feldwebel Hugo Bauer and his gunner Uffz Johannes Dittrich, he crashed to his death at Fassberg near Göttingen. The 'Viermotorenknacker' was no more.

As an indication of how many awards were given to one single Geschwader, let us consider the Geschwader in which Hauptmann Rudolf Sigmund served when he obtained his Ritterkreuz, Nachtjagd-geschwader 1. From 26 July 1940 until the end of the war, the Geschwader lost 135 officers and 541 non-coms and soldiers, distributed as follows:

	Officers	Other Ranks
Geschwaderstab	3	6
I/NJG1	35	118
II/NJG1	35	149
III/NJG1	33	154
IV/NJG1	29	114
Total	135	541

During this period it obtained 2,173 victories at night and 145 during the day, distributed as follows:

	Day	Night
Geschwaderstab	6	24
I/NJG1	—	585
II/NJG1	119	405
III/NJG1	7	343
IV/NJG1	13	816
Total	145	2,173

For these losses and these results, the NJG1 members obtained:
One German Cross in Silver; 81 German Cross in Gold; 36 Knight's Cross; 16 Oak Leaves to the Knight's Cross; two Oak Leaves with Swords to the Knight's Cross; one Oak Leaves with Sword and Diamonds to the Knight's Cross.

206

Two Bf110E-1s of I/NJG3. The unit stayed at various airfields in Germany, but in February 1941 the 1st Staffel was sent to the Mediterranean area, staying there until October of the same year. The 2nd, to which the aircraft depicted belong, and the 3rd Staffel remained in the home-country. After the 1st Staffel rejoined the parent unit again, the Gruppe saw action over the North German coastal area, together with the other Gruppen of the Geschwader. *Bundesarchiv*

The Survivor

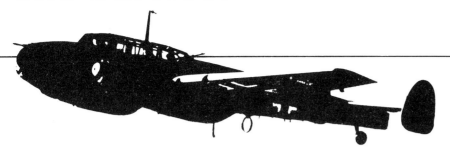

Of the more than 6,000 Bf110s that were built, only one fully intact example survives today. It is BF110G-4/R3, WNr 730301, coded D5+RL, which at the end of World War 2 was serving with I/NJG3. This is its history after the war:

- Captured at Grove in 1945.
- Ferried from Schleswig to RAE Farnborough, on 3 August 1945.
- Allotted serial AM34.
- To 6 MU Brize Norton, on 5 September 1945.
- To 76 MU Wroughton, for museum storage on 14 August 1946.
- To German AF Equipment Centre, 4 MU Stanmore Park, by 1949.
- To RAF Andover.
- To RAF Biggin Hill.
- To RAF Henlow.
- To RAF St Athan for restoration in August 1973.
- Allotted serial 8479M
- To Battle of Britain Museum, Hendon, in 1978.
- Now on permanent public display at Battle of Britain Museum.

Asked about the unusual camouflage scheme of the aircraft in question, Mr Michael A. Fopp, then keeper of the Battle of Britain Museum, said: 'Its restoration was undertaken by Royal Air Force personnel at St Athan and they informed me that the markings painted on this aircraft were the nearest they could get to those markings they discovered underneath the Royal Air Force paint scheme that had been applied.'

Also on display at the Battle of Britain Museum is the only Victoria Cross to be awarded to a fighter pilot during World War 2 from the 32 VCs awarded to airmen during that conflict. It was not awarded for any high tally of air combat victories but for a specific act of individual courage shown by a pilot during his first-ever experience of aerial combat . . . against a Bf110.

On Friday 16 August 1940, acting Flight Commander Eric James Brindley Nicolson of No 249 Squadron was hit during an aerial combat in his Hurricane. Fire from Bf109s drove a shard of perspex through his left eyelid, another hit smashed through the cockpit side tearing his right trouser leg to shreds while another hit the heel of his left shoe and wounded him in the foot. As if

207
This is the only fully intact Bf110 of the 6,150 built which survives to this day. The aircraft — on display at the Battle of Britain Museum at Hendon, England — once belonged to I/NJG3. It is a Bf110G-4/R3, coded D5+RL, with WNr 730301.
Beneath both wings the Rüstsatz B2 — two 300-litre fuel tanks — are visible. The exhaust flame dampers are still in place on each side of both engines. Mounted on the nose section of the aircraft are the antennas of the FuG220B Lichtenstein SN2 radar.

this was not enough another hit set his fuselage petrol tank afire. While a real furnace of fuel flames was erupting in front of him and with blood obscuring vision from his left eye and with the pain in his leg, Nicolson fired at a Bf110 that suddenly appeared in his gunsight. He managed to bale out afterwards and while hanging in his parachute he was wounded once more when some trigger-happy volunteer soldier hit him in the buttock with a 12-bore shot. On 15 November 1940 while still recovering from his wounds he was awarded the Victoria Cross. He was killed on 2 May 1945 while flying as a passenger in a Liberator of No 355 Squadron which crashed south of Calcutta in the open sea. His body was never found.

Flt Lt Nicolson's Victoria Cross was auctioned off in April 1983. The Battle of Britain Museum paid £110,000 for this medal and Nicolson's other awards and decorations and various other pieces of memorabilia from the family. It was the intention to create an individual exhibition dedicated to Flt Lt Nicolson which will display all these items but the medals have been on display since the day after the auction. The decision to auction off the VC was taken by the family of Nicolson apparently as a protest against the low pensions paid out to war-widows. They receive only £168 every month. Sic transit. . .

208

Although the radio mast has disappeared, the aircraft has the rarely seen combination of a radio mast for the Zielflugempfänger EZ2 and the Funklande-Empfänger EB1, together with a D/F loop antenna for the FuG16Z, both of them mounted on top of the cockpit.

It is of interest to note that this aircraft was flown by Capt Eric Brown CBE, DSC, AFC, RN, at the RAE Farnborough, in 1945.